THE PRINCIPLES OF
ENGLISH VERSIFICATION

BY

PAULL FRANKLIN BAUM

CAMBRIDGE

HARVARD UNIVERSITY PRESS

LONDON: HUMPHREY MILFORD

OXFORD UNIVERSITY PRESS

1923

PRINTED AT THE HARVARD UNIVERSITY PRESS
CAMBRIDGE, MASS., U. S. A.

TO

C. H. N. B.

PREFACE

MOST of the older discussions of English versification labored under two difficulties: an undue
adherence to the traditions of Greek and Latin prosody
more or less perfectly understood, and an exaggerated
formalism. But recently the interest and excitement
(now happily abated) over free-verse have reopened
the old questions and let in upon them not a little
light. Even today, however, a great deal of metrical
analysis has wrecked itself on the visible rocks of a
false accuracy, and it is therefore not only out of caution but also out of mere common sense that we should
eschew the arbitrary, even at the risk of vagueness
and an 'unscientific' admission of uncertainty. For
the only great and annihilating danger of writing on
versification is dogmatism. Our theorists, both old
and new, are first tempted and then possessed with
their theories — all else becoming wrong and intoler-
able. In the following pages I have perhaps erred in
a too frequent insistence on doubts and perplexities;
perhaps also, on occasion, in a too plain statement of
opinion where judgments are bound to differ — *sic
se res habent.*

Now it is plain that rhythm is one of the ultimate
facts of nature and one of the universal principles of

art; and thus versification, which is the study of the rhythms of verse, is both a science and an art. But it differs from the other sciences in that its phenomena are not 'regular' and reducible to law, but varying and subject to the dictates, even the whims, of genius; inasmuch as every poem involves a fresh fiat of creation. Of course, no poet when he is composing, either in the traditional "fine frenzy" or in the more sober process of revision, thinks of prosody as a science, or perhaps thinks of it at all. If he did he would go mad, and produce nothing. But the phenomena remain, nevertheless, and the analysis of them becomes for us a science.

This analysis has what Bacon would call two inconveniences. The first is complexity. The various ways in which the formal rhythms of verse combine with the infinitely modulated rhythms of natural prose produce a resultant which is complicated to the last degree and which almost precludes orderly exposition. No system has been devised to express it. The simpler ones fail through omission of important difficulties, the more elaborate totter under their own weight. And thus the Gentle Reader is either beguiled by false prophets — looks up and is not fed — or loses heart and saves himself by flight. There is, to be sure, an arcanum of prosodic theory which is the province of specialists. It has its place in the scheme of things; but it is no more necessary for the genuine enjoyment of Milton (or the 'moderns') than a knowledge of the formulae for calculating the parallax of Alpha Leonis is necessary for enjoying the pillared firmament. We must then compromise with a system which reveals the existence of all the phenomena and tries to suggest their interrelated workings.

The other inconvenience is that of seeming to deny the real poetry by our preoccupation with its metrical expression. "Under pretence that we want to study it more in detail, we pulverize the statue." This is an old charge, and our answer is easy. For, however it may be with the statue, a poem is never pulverized; it is still there on the page! No amount of analyzing can injure the poem. It we think it has injured us, even then we err, and need only recall our natural aversion to hard labor. In nearly every instance it was the work and not the analysis that bothered us.

This is a small book and therefore not exhaustive. And since it is as elementary, especially in the treatment of the principles of rhythm, as is consistent with a measure of thoroughness, the apparatus of mere learning has been suppressed, even where it might perhaps seem needed, as in footnote references to the scientific investigations on which part of the text is based. I have consulted and used, of course, all the books and articles I could find that had anything of value to offer; but I have rarely cited them, not because I wish to conceal my indebtedness, but because there is no room for elaborate documentation in such a book as this. On the other hand, I owe a very great deal, both directly and indirectly, to Professor Bliss Perry — although my manuscript was finished before I saw his Study of Poetry; and this debt I wish to acknowledge most fully and gratefully.

In lieu of a formal bibliography, I think it sufficient
(in addition to the footnotes that occur in their proper
place) to refer the reader to the larger works of
Schipper and Saintsbury, to the smaller volumes of
Professor Perry and Professor R. M. Alden, and particularly to Mr. T. S. Omond's English Metrists, 1921.

P. F. B.

CONTENTS

PAGE

I. RHYTHM 3

II. RHYTHM OF PROSE AND VERSE 22

III. METRE 49

IV. METRICAL FORMS:

    1. THE LINE 69

    2. THE STANZA 88

    3. BLANK VERSE 133

    4. FREE-VERSE 150

    5. EXOTIC FORMS 159

V. MELODY, HARMONY, AND MODULATION . . . 165

GLOSSARIAL INDEX 207

ENGLISH VERSIFICATION

CHAPTER I

RHYTHM

RHYTHM, in its simplest sense, is measured motion; but by various natural extensions of meaning the word has come to be used almost as a synonym of regularity of variation. Whatever changes or alternates according to a recognizable system is said to be rhythmic, to possess rhythm. In this sense, rhythm is one of the universal principles of nature. We find it in the stripes of the zebra, the indentation of leaves, the series of teeth or of crystals, the curves of the horizon; in the tides, the phases of the moon, the rising and setting of the sun, the recurrence of seasons, the revolutions of planets; in the vibrations of color, sound, and heat; in breathing, the throbbing of the pulse, the stride of walking. All action and reaction whatever is rhythmic, both in nature and in man. "Rhythm is the rule with Nature," said Tyndall; "she abhors uniformity more than she does a vacuum." So deeprooted, in truth, is this principle, that we imagine it and feel it where it does not exist, as in the clicking of a typewriter. Thus there is both an *objective rhythm*, which actually exists as rhythm, and a *subjective rhythm*, which is only the feeling of regularity resulting from a natural tendency of the mind to 'organize' any irregularity that we meet.

There are two fundamental forms of rhythm, though these are not altogether mutually exclusive, (1) spatial, and (2) temporal.

Spatial Rhythms. The simplest spatial rhythm is a series of equidistant points —

. . . .

More complex forms are the succession of repeated designs in mouldings and wainscotings (for example, the alternation of egg and dart), the series of windows in a wall, or of the columns of a Greek temple, or of the black and white keys of a piano. Still more complex is the balanced arrangement of straight lines and curves in a geometrical design, as in certain Oriental rugs or the Gothic rose windows. And probably the most complex spatial rhythms are those of the façades of great buildings like the Gothic cathedrals or St. Mark's of Venice, where only the trained eye perceives the subtleties of alternation and balance.

Temporal Rhythms. Temporal rhythms, apart from those of planetary motion, the alternation of seasons, and the like (which are called rhythmic by a metaphorical extension of the term), manifest themselves to us as phenomena of sound; hence the two concepts time-rhythm and sound-rhythm are commonly thought of as one and the same.

The simplest form is the tick-tick-tick of a watch or metronome. But such mechanical regularity is comparatively rare, and in general the temporal rhythms are all highly complex composites of sounds and silences. Their highest manifestations are music and language. The rhythm of language, and *a fortiori* that of verse, is therefore primarily a temporal or sound rhythm, and as such is the particular subject of the following pages.

Combinations. Language, however, when addressed to the eye rather than to the ear, that is, when written or printed rather than spoken, is partly a spatial phenomenon; and, as will appear presently, the arrangement of words and sentences on the formal page is a real factor in the rhythm of verse. Moreover, most of the rhythms of motion, such as walking, the ebb and flow of tides, the breaking of waves on the beach, are composites of temporal and spatial.[1]

Sound Rhythm. These elementary generalizations must be narrowed now to the special phenomena of sound, and then still more particularly to the sounds of language.

All musical tones, including the phonetic sounds of words, have four characteristics: pitch, loudness or intensity, quality or tone-color, and duration. The last, of course, needs no definition.

Pitch is dependent on the number of vibrations per second. The greater the number of vibrations, the higher the pitch and the more 'acute' the tone. The

---

[1] One hears sometimes of 'rhythmic thought' and 'rhythmic feeling.' This is merely a further extension or metaphorical usage of the term. In Othello, for instance, there is a more or less regular alternation of the feelings of purity and jealousy, and of tragedy and comedy. In some of the Dialogues of Plato there is a certain rhythm of thought. This usage is fairly included in the Oxford Dictionary's definition: "movement marked by the regulated succession of strong and weak elements, or of opposite or different conditions."

lowest pitch recognizable as a tone (as distinguished from noise) is 8 vibrations a second; the highest pitch the ear can hear is between 20,000 and 30,000 a second. In normal English speech among adults the voice ranges from about 100 to 300 vibrations, but in animated speaking this range is greatly increased.

Loudness is a comparative term for the strength of the sensation of sound in the ear. It is determined by the energy or intensity of the vibrations and varies (technically speaking) as the product of the square of the frequency and the square of the amplitude ($I = n^2A^2$). But for ordinary purposes it is sufficient to regard loudness and intensity as the same. The distinction, however, is clear in common practice; for whether one says "father" loudly or quietly, there is a relatively greater intensity of sound in the first syllable than in the second. In speech this intensity is called *accent* or *stress*.

The third characteristic, variously called *quality*, *timbre*, *tone-quality*, *tone-color*, is that which distinguishes sounds of the same loudness and pitch produced by different instruments or voices. It is the result of the combination of the partial tones of a sound, that is, of the fundamental and its overtones. In music, tone-quality is of the utmost importance, but as an element of speech rhythm it is practically non-existent, and may be wholly neglected, though it plays, of course, a prominent part in the oral reading of different persons.[1]

---

[1] There is, however, another phenomenon (to be discussed later) called by the same name, ' tone-color,' but having only a metaphorical

What is the relation of these physical attributes of sound to sound rhythm? The answer lies in a closer examination of the nature of rhythm, especially as it concerns the rhythm of speech.

Rhythm means measured flow or succession. Now first, in order that any succession may be measured, there must be something recognizable which distinguishes one unit from the next. In spatial rhythms the point of division is almost always easily perceived; hence the greater difficulty of analyzing the simplest time-rhythms as compared with the most complex space-rhythms. Moreover, the basis of measurement, that by which the 'distance' between any point of division and that which follows it is determined, must, by definition, be duration of time. Suppose, however, that the time-distance between successive points of emphasis or division is equal, is the rhythm therefore necessarily regular? No, because the points of emphasis themselves may vary in force or energy. Thus if in the following scheme (′ = point of emphasis; — = equal time-distance):

$$′ - ′ - ′ - ′ - ′ - ′ - \text{etc.}$$

every ′ is not of the same value, the result might be (″ = twice as much emphasis as ′; ‴ = three times as much):

$$″ - ′ - ‴ - ″ - ″ - ‴ - \text{etc.}$$

relation to it. Many words — *father, soul, ineluctable,* for example — have emotional associations which stand to the literal meaning somewhat like overtones to the fundamental. This tone-quality of language is one of the primary and most significant sources of poetical effect, but it should never be confused with the musical term on which it is patterned.

and this could not be called regular. A simple illustration of this is the difference in music between ¾ time, where we count 1′ 2 3, 1′ 2 3, 1′ 2 3 and 6/4 or 6/8 time, where we count 1″ 2 3 4′ 5 6, 1″ 2 3 4′ 5 6. Furthermore, apart from any question of force or energy applied in the production of a sound, it is clear that high notes seem to possess a greater strength than low notes, and must therefore be recognized as an element in rhythmic emphasis. For example, if the following series of notes were sounded on a piano, and each struck with equal force —

 etc.

a certain 'accent' would probably be felt on the *e* which was not felt on the *a*. And it is well known that shrill sounds and high-pitched voices carry farther and *seem louder* than others.

In the simplest kind of temporal rhythm, therefore, where the beats are, say, drum-taps of equal force, the primary element is time. But if there is the added complication of drum-taps of unequal force, the element of comparative stress must be reckoned with. And if, finally, the drum-taps are not in the same key (say, on kettledrums differently tuned), then the further element of comparative pitch must be considered as a possible point of emphasis. In a word, pitch may sometimes be substituted for stress.

In music rhythmic units may be marked by differences in tone-quality as well, and thus the potential complexity is greatly increased; but in spoken language, as has been said, this element of rhythm is negligible. In speech-rhythm, however, the three conditions of time, stress, and pitch are always present, and therefore no consideration of either prose rhythm or verse can hope to be complete or adequate which neglects any one of them or the possibilities of their permutations and combinations. And it is precisely here that many treatments of the rhythm of language have revealed their weakness: they have excluded pitch usually, and often either stress or time. They have tried to build up a whole system of prosody sometimes on a foundation of stress alone, sometimes of time alone. The reason for this failure is simple, and it is also a warning. Any attempt to reckon with these three forces, each of which is extremely variable, not only among different individuals but in the same person at different times — any attempt to analyze these elements and observe, as well, their mutual influences and combined effects, is bound to result in a complication of details that almost defies expression or comprehension. The danger is as great as the difficulty. But nothing can ever be gained by the sort of simplification which disregards existent and relevant facts. It is to be confessed at once, however, that one cannot hope to answer in any really adequate way all or even most of the questions that arise. The best that can be expected is a thorough recognition of the complexity, together with some recognition of the component difficulties.

Moreover, only a part of the problem has been stated thus far. Not only is all spoken language the resultant of the subjectively variable forces of time, stress, and pitch, but these three forces are themselves subject to and intimately affected by the thought and emotion which they express. Though educated persons probably receive the phenomena of language more frequently through the eye than through the ear, it is true that words are, in the first instance, sounds, of which the printed or written marks are but conventional symbols. And these symbols and the sounds which they represent have other values also, logical or intellectual and emotional values. Language is therefore a compound instrument of both sound and meaning, and speech-rhythm, in its fullest sense, is the composite resultant of the attributes of sound (duration, intensity, and pitch) modified by the logical and emotional content of the words and phrases which they represent.

For example, utter the words: "A house is my fire," and observe the comparative duration of time in the pronunciation of each word, the comparative stress, and the relative pitch (e. g. of *a* and *fire*). Now rearrange these nearly meaningless syllables: "My house is afire." Observe the differences, some slight and some well marked, in time, stress, and pitch. Then consider the different emotional coloring this sentence might have and the different results on time, stress, and pitch in utterance, if, say, the house contains all that you hold most precious and there is no chance of rescue; or if, on the other hand, the house is worthless and you are glad to see it destroyed. And even here the matter is comparatively simple; for in reading the

following sentence from Walter Pater, note the manifold variations in your own utterance of it at different
times and imagine how it would be read by a person of
dull sensibilities, by one of keen poetic feeling, and
finally by one who recalled its context and on that
account could enjoy its fullest richness: "It is the
landscape, not of dreams or of fancy, but of places far
withdrawn, and hours selected from a thousand with a
miracle of finesse." [1]

The last step of the complication, which can only be
indicated here, and will be developed in a later chapter,
comes with the mutual adjustment of the natural prose
rhythm and the metrical pattern of the verse. Such a
sentence as the following has its own peculiar rhythms:
"And, as imagination bodies forth the forms of things
unknown, the poet's pen turns them to shapes, and
gives to airy nothing a local habitation and a name."
Now read it as verse, and the rhythms are different;
both the meaning and the music are enhanced.

[1] Walter Pater, "Leonardo da Vinci," in The Renaissance. For an account of scientific experiments on the time and stress rhythm of this sentence, see W. M. Patterson, The Rhythm of Prose, New York, 1916,
ch. iv. An idea of the complexity may be obtained from Patterson's
attempt to indicate it by musical notation:

And as imagination bodies forth
The forms of things unknown, the poet's pen
Turns them to shapes, and gives to airy nothing
A local habitation and a name.
                    SHAKESPEARE, Midsummer Night's Dream, V, i.

These then are the problems and the difficulties. The solutions can be only partial and tentative, but they are the best we are able to obtain with our present knowledge and our present capabilities of analysis. As science today has advanced in accuracy of knowledge and understanding of the facts of nature far beyond the powers of our ancestors to imagine, so in the future psychologists may, and let us hope will, enable us to comprehend the subtleties of metrical rhythm beyond our present power. Yet there will always remain, since the ever-inexplicable element of genius is a necessary part of all art, a portion which no science can describe or analyze.

The Psychology of Rhythm. That nearly all persons have a definite sense of rhythm, though sometimes latent because of defective education, is a familiar fact. The origin and source of this sense is a matter of uncertainty and dispute. The regular beating of the heart, the regular alternation of inhaling and exhaling, the regular motions of walking, all these unconscious or semi-conscious activities of the body have been suggested; and they doubtless have a concomitant if not a direct influence on the rhythmic sense. Certainly there is an intimate relation between the heart action and breath rate and the external stimulus of certain rhythmic forces, as is shown by the tendency of the pulse and breath to adapt their *tempo* to the beat of fast or slow music. But this can hardly be the whole explanation. More important, from the psychological point of view, is doubtless the alternation of effort and fatigue which characterizes our mental as well as physical actions. A period of concentrated attention is at once followed by a period of indifference; the attention flags, wearies, and must be recuperated by a pause, just as the muscular effort of hand or arm. In truth, the muscles of the eye play a real part in the alternations of effort and rest in reading. The immediate application of this psychological fact to the temporal rhythms has been clearly phrased by the French metrist, M. Verrier:

I hear the first beat of a piece of music or of a verse, and, my attention immediately awakened, I await the second. At the end of a certain time — that is, when the expense of energy demanded has reached a certain degree — this second beat strikes my ear. Then I expect to hear the third when the dynamic sense of attention shall indicate an equal expense of energy, that is, at the end of an equal interval of time. Thus, by means of sensation and of memory of the amount of energy expended in the attention each time, I can perceive the equality of time-interval of the rhythmic units. Once this effort of attention becomes definite and fixed, it repeats itself instinctively and mechanically — by reflex action, so to say, like that of walking when we are accustomed to a stride of a given length and rapidity. Here we have truly a sort of metronome which will beat out the rhythm according as we regulate it. And it goes without saying that with this we can not only note the rhythm in our songs or spoken verse or movements, but also perceive it in the sounds and movements of other persons and other things.

This metronome of attention functions, indeed, still more simply. With attention, as with all the psycho-physiological processes, effort alternates with rest: it grows stronger and weaker, contracts and expands in turn. This *pulse of attention* varies in different persons according to the peculiar rhythm of the organism. In the same person, under normal conditions, it remains nearly constant. It is always subject to modification by the psycho-physiological conditions of the moment, especially by the emotions and by external circumstances. In a series of identical equidistant stresses, those which coincide with the pulse of attention seem the stronger: this is what is called *subjective rhythm*. Since this coincidence is nearly always somewhat inexact, there results an easy accommodation of the pulse of attention, although even in the subjective rhythm there has already occurred an objective influence capable of affecting us sensibly.[1]

Thus we have always at hand both a more or less efficient bodily metronome in the pulse and in respiration, and also a "cerebral metronome" capable not only of easy adjustment to different rates of speed but also of that subtlest of modulations which psychologists call the 'elastic unit,' and which musicians, though not so definitely or surely, recognize as *tempo rubato*.

The sense of rhythm, as has been said, differs remarkably in different individuals — just as the sense of touch, of smell, of hearing.[2] To some, rhythm appears chiefly as a series of points of emphasis or stresses alternating with points of less emphasis or of none at all; such are called, in scientific jargon, ' stressers.' To others the principal characteristic of rhythm is the time intervals; such are called ' timers.' But this is a practical, not a philosophical distinction. For it is the

[1] Paul Verrier, Essai sur les Principes de la Métrique Anglaise (Paris, 1909), Deuxieme Partie, Livre II, ch. x, pp. 56, 57; and cf. p. 90, n. 1.

[2] A simple experiment will illustrate this. Place two persons back to back, so that they cannot see each other, and have them beat time to an audible melody; as soon as the music ceases they will begin to beat differently. (Verrier, II, p. 65.) The difficulty of keeping even a trained orchestra playing together illustrates the same fact.

succession of points of emphasis which even the most aggressive stresser feels as rhythmic; and succession implies and involves a temporal element. The stresser's only difficulty is to feel the approximate *equality* of the interval. The essential thing, however, is to understand that, while time is the foundation of speech-rhythm, stress is its universal adjunct and concomitant.[1]

The explanation of this duality is simple. A series of identical tones

 etc.

contains a simple objective rhythm. The pronounced timer will feel it clearly; the extreme stresser will not. Change the series to

 etc.,

or

 etc.,

and both will feel it; for in the last example both time and stress are obvious, and in the other the longer notes of the series produce the effect of stress.[2] Most persons, therefore, with a greater or less degree of consciousness, allow their physical or cerebral metronome to affect the simple

 etc.,

---

[1] "If rhythm means anything to the average individual, it means motor response and a sense of organized time." Patterson, p. 14.

[2] Musicians often ' dot ' a note for the sake of emphasizing the accent, especially in orchestral music and with such instruments as the flute, where variations of stress are difficult to produce.

so that they hear or feel either

or

It is thus that the clock says tick-*tock*, tick-*tock*, the locomotive *chu*-chu, *chu*-chu. Timers are in the minority.

A converse phenomenon of the subjective introduction of stress into a series of identical tones at equal intervals is the subjective ' organization ' of a series of irregular beats. Some do this more easily and naturally than others, but the tendency is present in all who are not absolutely rhythm-deaf. The "minute drops from off the eaves" beat out a tune, the typewriter develops a monotonous song, the public speaker ' gets his stride ' and continues in a sing-song.

Thus, when there are equal intervals but stress is absent, we more or less unconsciously supply it; when there are distinct stresses at irregular intervals we organize them into approximately regular intervals. We have in us by instinct and by development both the *ability* and also the *need* to draw forth rhythm wherever it is latent. Rhythm becomes one of our physical and mental pleasures, manifest in primitive dancing and balladry, sailors' chanteys, and the simple *heave-ho*'s of concerted labor. It induces economy of effort, and so makes work lighter; and it has, though perhaps not always, a certain æsthetic value, in making labor more interesting as well as easier. It is one of the attributes of the god we worship under the name of System.

Coördination, Syncopation, Substitution. The processes of the subjective organization of rhythm may
best be explained under the heads of coördination, syncopation, and substitution. Their application to the
particular problems of verse will be apparent at once,
and will, in fact, constitute the bulk of the following
pages.

Coördination has two aspects, according as it is
thought of simply as an existing fact or as a process.
In the former sense it is the agreement or coincidence
(or the perception of agreement or coincidence) between the simple normal recurrence of beats and the
actual or predetermined pattern. Thus in the lines

> And swims, or sinks, or wades, or creeps, or flies,
>   MILTON, Paradise Lost, II, 950

> A sable, silent, solemn forest stood,
>   THOMSON, Castle of Indolence, st. 5

the ' natural ' beat of the words uttered in the most
natural and reasonable manner coincides with the
' artificial ' beat of the metrical line.

On the other hand, coördination is the process which
results in one's reduction of irregular beats to an approximately regular series. When we hear a haphaz-
ard succession of drum-taps or the irregular click-click
of the typewriter, most of us soon begin to feel a certain orderly arrangement, a rhythmical *swing* in the
repeated sounds, a grouping according to a sort of unit
which recurs with nearly equal intervals. The units
are not absolutely equal, but are elastic, allowing of
some contraction and expansion; yet they are so nearly
equal, or we feel them so, that the series seems regular.

Now this process of coördination involves two activities, syncopation and substitution. The workings of both are highly complex and somewhat uncertain; they differ greatly in different individuals, and when analyzed scientifically seem to produce more difficulties than they explain. But fortunately the outstanding ideas are beyond dispute, and detailed examination can properly be left to the scientists.

Syncopation is the union, or the perception of the union, of two or more rhythmic patterns.[1] A familiar example is perhaps the ' three against two ' in music, where one hand follows a *tum*-te-te, *ium*-te-te rhythm, the other a *tum*-te, *tum*-te. This complexity, which strikes us as sophisticated subtlety and is not always easy to reproduce, is in fact both simple and familiar to the untutored savage. We must remember that the evolution of language and of music has been for the more part in the direction of greater simplicity of structure. Primitive music, as we find it in the undeveloped Indians and Australasians, is often too complex to be expressed by our regular notation. Another familiar example of syncopation is the negro dance, in which the "dancer taps with his feet just half-way between

---

[1] Cf. Patterson, p. 3, " . . . the possibility of preserving a certain series of time intervals, but of changing in various ways the nature of the motions or sensations that mark the beats." This may be tested by a simple experiment. With the foot or finger tap evenly, regularly, and rather rapidly. Without changing the regularity of the tapping, but merely by a mental readjustment, the beats may be felt as *tum*-te, *tum*-te, *tum*-te (or te-*tum*, etc.) or as *tum*-te-te, *tum*-te-te, *tum*-te-te (or te-te-*tum*, etc.), or even as *tum*-te-te-te, *tum*-te-te-te (or te-te-te-*tum*, etc.). It is but a step from this successive perception of various rhythms from the same objective source to a combined and simultaneous perception of them.

the hand-claps of those who are accompanying his per-
formance."[1] And of course the commonest example
is the strongly marked syncopation of ragtime.[2]

In prose, this syncopation is evident in the apparent
recognition, and even reproduction in reading aloud, of
a regularity of rhythm where none really exists; as
when protracted reading or listening develops or seems
to develop a monotonous sing-song. But this phenomenon cannot be explained briefly, and the details
must be omitted here.[3] In verse also syncopation frequently occurs, though it is seldom recognized except
as an 'irregularity.' In the following lines of Paradise
Lost the first two coincide pretty closely with the normal beats of the measure; while in the third line the
series is an entirely different one.

> So Satan spake, and him Beelzebub
> Thus answered: " Leader of those armies bright,
> *Which but th' Omnipotent none could have foil'd.* . . ."
>
> MILTON, Paradise Lost, I, 271–273.

Here to stress distinctly *but, -tent, could* utterly ruins
both the meaning and the music of the line: to utter
the words as if they were ordinary prose would preserve the meaning, but destroy the verse-movement.
In Milton's ear, however, and in ours if we do not re-
sist, there is a subtle syncopation of four beats against
five. (Of course syncopation alone does not explain the

---

[1] Patterson, p. xx, n. 3.

[2] Experiments have shown that with a little practice one can learn to
beat five against seven, and thus actually though unconsciously count in
thirty-fives. (Patterson, p. 6.)

[3] Those who are interested will find the scientific experiments discussed in Patterson, ch. i and Appendix III.

rhythm of this line.) A most startling syncopation is ventured by Milton in Samson Agonistes (1071–72):

> I less conjecture than when first I saw
> *The sumptuous Dâlila floating this way.*

Substitution is simpler. It merely means recognizing the equivalence, and therefore the possibility of interchange, of a long interval with two or more shorter intervals whose sum equals the one long. That is, in music two quarter-notes are equal to a half-note, and they may be anywhere substituted one for the other; or a dotted half-note equal three quarter-notes, etc. In verse it means that three syllables (or one, or even four) may be substituted for the normal two syllables of a foot if the three (or one or four) are uttered in approximately the same period of time.

The term *substitution*, however, may be used in a larger sense. Thus far only the purely temporal element of the rhythm has been thought of. When the two others, stress and pitch, are recalled, it becomes clear that another sort of substitution is both possible and usual, namely, that of either pitch or stress for duration. In other words, the groups that make up a rhythmic series may be determined or marked off by emphasis of pitch or emphasis of stress as well as by duration of time. In fact, it is from this habitual interplay of the three elements that most of the complexity of metre arises; as it is the failure to recognize this substitution which has given the older prosodies much of their false simplicity and their mechanical barrenness.

Summary. The fundamental problems of versification are all involved in the principles of rhythm, especially the temporal rhythm of language. The rhythm of both prose and verse is a resultant of the three attributes of sound: stress, duration, and pitch (the first two being usually the determining elements, the third an accessory element) modified by the thought and emotion of the words. The feeling for this rhythm, or perception of it, has both physical and psychological explanations, and varies considerably among individuals, some being 'timers,' others 'stressers,' apparently by natural endowment. The processes of our perception of rhythm are those of coördination, or partly subjective reduction of actual 'irregularities' to a standard of 'regularity'; this reduction being accomplished mainly by syncopation and substitution.

CHAPTER II

RHYTHM OF PROSE AND VERSE

IT is clear now that all language is more or less definitely rhythmical; and that the two fundamental and determining elements of speech-rhythm are time and stress. It is clear also that the essential thing in our perception of rhythm is the experience or recognition of groups, these groups being themselves distinguished and set off by stress and time. When there is an easily felt regularity of the groups, when the alternation of stress and unstress and the approximate equality of the time intervals are fairly apparent, then the rhythm is simple. When the regularity is not obvious, the rhythm is complex, but none the less existent and pleasing.[1] In other words, the character of language rhythm is determined by the relative proportion of coincidence and syncopation. In verse, coincidence preponderates; in prose, syncopation (and substitution). Between absolute coincidence, moreover, and the freest possible syncopation and substitution, infinite gradations are possible; and many passages indeed lie so close to the boundary between recognizable preponderance of the one or of the other that it is difficult to say *this* is verse, *that* is prose.

[1] When no organization of the irregularity is possible, the language is unrhythmical; and such, of course, is often the case in bad prose and bad verse.

Various standards and conventions enter into the decision.

For practical convenience three main sorts of rhythmic prose may be distinguished: (1) *characteristic prose*, or that in which no regularity (coincidence) is easily appreciable; (2) *cadenced prose*, or that in which the regularity is perceptible, but unobtrusive, and (3) *metrical prose*, or that in which the regularity is so noticeable as to be unpleasing. No very clear lines can be drawn; nor should one try to classify more than brief passages in one group or another. And, obviously, longer selections will combine two or more sorts in succession. A few examples will serve to show what is meant.

Characteristic Prose. No prose, as has been said above, is without rhythmic curves; but the best prose, that which always keeps in view the best ideals of prose, carefully avoids consecutive repetitions of the same rhythmic patterns. It is the distinction of verse to follow a chosen pattern, with due regard to the artistic principles of variety and uniformity; it is the distinction of prose to accomplish its object, whether artistic or utilitarian, without encroaching on the boundaries of its neighbor. Prose may be as 'poetic,' as charged with powerful emotion, as possible, but it remains true prose only when it refuses to borrow aids from the characteristic excellences of verse.

To be sure, it is not always easy to avoid regular patterns in writing the most ordinary prose. They come uncalled; they seem to be inherent in the language. Here is, chosen casually, the first sentence of a current news item, written surely without artistic elaboration, and subjected, moreover, to the uncertainties of cable transmission. It was no doubt farthest from the correspondent's intention to write ' numerous ' prose; but notice how the sentence may be divided into a series of rhythmic groups of two stresses each, with a fairly regular number of accompanying unstressed syllables:

A general mobilization | in Syria has been ordered | as a reply to the French | ultimatum to King Feisal | that he acquiesce in the French | mandate for Syria, | according to a dispatch | to the London Times | from Jerusalem.

No one would read the sentence with a very clear feeling of this definite movement; in fact, to do so rather obscures the meaning. But the potential rhythm is there, and the reader with a keen rhythmic sense will be to some extent aware of it.

Again, there is in the following sentence from Disraeli's Endymion a latent rhythm which actually affects the purely logical manner of reading it:

She persisted in her dreams of riding upon elephants.

Here one almost inevitably pauses after *dreams* (or prolongs the word beyond its natural length), though there is no logical reason for doing so. Why? Partly, at least, because *persisted in her dreams* and *of riding upon el-* have the same ' swing,' and the parallelism of mere sound seems to require the pause.

For these reasons, then, among others, the most ' natural ' spontaneous and straightforward prose is not always the best. Study and careful revision are necessary in order to avoid an awkward and unpleasant monotony of rhythmic repetition, and at the same time obtain a flow of sound which will form a just musical accompaniment to the ideas expressed. Only the great prose masters have done this with complete success. Of the three following examples the first is from Bacon; the second is from Milton, who as a poet might have been expected to fall into metre while writing emotional prose; the third is from Walter Pater — the famous translation into words of the Mona Lisa painted by Leonardo da Vinci. The first is elaborate but unaffected, the second is probably spontaneous, the third highly studied.

This kind of degenerate learning did chiefly reign amongst the schoolmen: who having sharp and strong wits, and abundance of leisure, and small variety of reading, but their wits being shut up in the cells of a few authors (chiefly Aristotle their dictator) as their persons were shut up in the cells of monasteries and colleges, and knowing little history, either of nature or time, did out of no great quantity of matter and infinite agitation of wit spin out unto us those laborious webs of learning which are extant in their books. For the wit and mind of man, if it work upon matter, which is the contemplation of the creatures of God, worketh according to the stuff and is limited thereby; but if it work upon itself, as the spider worketh his web, then it is endless, and brings forth indeed cobwebs of learning, admirable for the fineness of thread and work, but of no substance or profit.

Advancement of Learning, Bk. I, iv, 5.

Truth indeed came once into the world with her divine Master, and was a perfect shape most glorious to look on; but when he ascended, and his Apostles after him were laid asleep, then straight arose a wicked race of deceivers, who, as that story goes of the Egyptian Typhon with his conspirators how they dealt with the good Osiris, took the virgin Truth, hewed her lovely form into a thousand pieces, and scattered them to the four winds. From that time ever since, the sad friends of Truth, such as durst appear, imitating the careful search that Isis made for the mangled body of Osiris, went up and down gathering up limb by limb still as they could find them.   Areopagitica.

Hers is the head upon which all "the ends of the world are come," and the eyelids are a little weary. It is a beauty wrought from within upon the flesh, the deposit, little cell by cell, of strange thoughts and fantastic reveries and exquisite passions. . . . She is older than the rocks among which she sits; like the vampire, she has been dead many times, and learned the secrets of the grave; and has been a diver in deep seas, and keeps their fallen day about her; and trafficked for strange webs with Eastern merchants: and, as Leda, was the mother of Helen of Troy, and, as Saint Anne, the mother of Mary; and all this has been to her but as the sound of lyres and flutes, and lives only in the delicacy with which it has moulded the changing lineaments, and tinged the eyelids and the hands.
              "Leonardo da Vinci," in The Renaissance.

Here no continuous patterns are recognizable, yet the whole is felt to be musically and appropriately rhythmic. In the next excerpt, however (from John Donne), and in many passages in the Authorized Version of the Psalms, of Job, of the Prophets, there is a visible balance of phrases and of clauses, a long undulating swing which one perceives at once, though only half consciously, and which approaches, if it does not actually possess, the intentional coincidence of cadenced prose.

If some king of the earth have so large an extent of dominion in north and south as that he hath winter and summer together in his dominions; so large an extent east and west as that he hath day and night together in his dominions, much more hath God mercy and justice together. He brought light out of darkness, not out of a lesser light; He can bring thy summer out of winter though thou have no spring; though in the ways of fortune, or of understanding, or conscience, thou have been benighted till now, wintered and frozen, smothered and stupefied till now, now God comes to thee, not as in the dawning of the day, not as in the bud of the spring, but as the sun at noon to illustrate all shadows, as the sheaves in harvest to fill all penuries. All occasions invite His mercies, and all times are His seasons.

Cadenced Prose. Cadenced prose is in English chiefly an historical phenomenon of the seventeenth century. It is part of the late Renaissance literary movement, when prose, after vaguely classic models, was held worth cultivating on its own account; and is in some degree a tempered afterglow of the crude brilliance of euphuistic balance and alliteration. It made no effort to conceal its definite rhythmic movements — rather, it gloried in them; but was always careful that they should not become monotonous or too palpable.

In the following examples the rhythmic units are for the sake of clearness indicated by separate lines, after the fashion of ' free-verse.' The passages should be read first with the line-division uppermost in the attention; then as continuous prose. The result of the second reading will be perhaps a fuller appreciation of the rhythmic richness of the sentences, both as to variety and uniformity. Sing-song and ' pounding ' are by all means to be deprecated.

(*a*) Simple two- and three-beat rhythms —

> O eloquent just
> and mighty Death!
> whom none could advise
> thou hast persuaded;
> what none hath dared
> thou hast done;

> and whom all the world hath flattered
> thou only hast cast out of the world
> and despised.
> Thou hast drawn together
> all the far-stretched greatness
> all the pride cruelty
> and ambition of man,
> and covered it all over
> with these two
> narrow words
> *Hic jacet.*
> Sir Walter Raleigh, History of the World, Bk. V, ch. vi.

(*b*) Simple three- and four-beat rhythms —

> They that have great intrigues of the world
> have a yoke upon their necks
> and cannot look back.
> And he that covets many things greedily
> and snatches at high things ambitiously
> that despises his neighbor proudly
> and bears his crosses peevishly
> or his prosperity impotently and passionately
> he that is a prodigal of his precious time
> and is tenacious and retentive of evil purposes
> is not a man disposed to this exercise:
> he hath reason to be afraid of his own memory
> and to dash his glass in pieces
> because it must needs represent to his own eyes
> an intolerable deformity.
> Jeremy Taylor, Holy Dying, ch. ii, sect. 2.

(*c*) Mainly two-beat rhythms —

> Now since these dead bones
> have already outlasted
> the living ones of Methuselah
> and in a yard under ground
> and thin walls of clay
> outworn all the strong
> and spacious buildings above it,

and quietly rested
under the drums and tramplings
of three conquests;
what Prince can promise
such diuturnity
unto his reliques
or might not gladly
        say
' Sic ego componi versus in ossa velim.'

SIR THOMAS BROWNE, Urn Burial, ch. v.

(d) Mainly three-beat rhythms —

What song the Syrens sang
or what name Achilles assumed
when he hid himself among women
        though puzzling questions
are not beyond all conjecture.
What time the persons of these ossuaries
entered the famous nations of the dead
and slept with princes and counsellors
might admit a wide solution.
But who were the proprietaries of these bones
or what bodies these ashes made up
were a question above antiquarism;
not to be resolved by man
nor easily perhaps by spirits
except we consult the provincial
guardians or tutelary Observators.

Ibid.

Metrical Prose. The above passages are daring, but greatly daring. So great is the subtlety, the variety, the art, that they never fail of their intended effect. They are justifiable because they justify themselves — partly by their lofty and dignified content, partly of course by their sheer artistry. But when the same thing is attempted by unskilful hands it fails ingloriously. We say it has "a palpable design upon us," and balk. Gibbon and Burke, as inheritors of the seventeenth-century tradition, sometimes fell into the error; Ruskin, with his ' poetical ' style, was sometimes guilty; but the worst and most conspicuous offenders were Dickens and Blackmore. Examples are abundant. Not all are equally unpleasant; the individual taste of some readers will approve passages which others will reject. With Dickens and Blackmore, however, the phenomenon approaches downright deliberate trickiness.

The calculation of profit in all such wars is false. On balancing the account of such wars, ten thousand hogsheads of sugar *are purchased at ten thousand times their price.* The blood of man should never *be shed but to redeem the blood of man.* It is well shed for our family, for our friends, for our God, for our country, for our kind. *The rest is vanity; the rest is crime.*

BURKE, Letters on a Regicide Peace, I.

When Death strikes down the innocent and young
for every fragile form from which he lets
    the panting spirit free
    a hundred virtues rise
in shapes of mercy, charity, and love,
    to walk the world and bless it.
Of every tear that sorrowing mortals shed
    on such green graves
    some good is born
some gentler nature comes.

DICKENS, Old Curiosity Shop, ch. 72.

"I wear the chain I forged in life," replied the Ghost,
"I made it link by link, and yard by yard."

DICKENS, Christmas Carol.

I cannot rest, I cannot stay,
I cannot linger anywhere.

Ibid.

Much they saw and far they went,
and many homes they visited,
but always with a happy end.

DICKENS, Christmas Carol.

But above the curved soft elbow,
where no room was for one cross word
(according to our proverb)
three sad gashes
edged with crimson
spoiled the flow of the pearly flesh.

BLACKMORE, Lorna Doone, ch. 38.

A peculiar instance of metrical prose, avowedly an experiment and fortunately (as most will think) not repeated, is the passage near the end of Kingsley's Westward Ho! Kingsley called it 'prose shaped into song.' The objection is simply that in such a situation song is out of place. Let prose do the legitimate work of prose; and when the intensity of feeling justifies song, let there be song. No hybrids, no cross-breeding — unless, as here, for purposes of experiment. Here is a part of the passage:

Then he took a locket from his bosom; and I heard him speak, Will, and he said: "Here's the picture of my fair and true lady; drink to her, Señors, all." Then he spoke to me, Will, and called me, right up through the oar-weed and the sea: "We have had a fair quarrel, Señor; it is time to be friends once more. My wife and your brother have forgiven me; so your honour takes no stain."

Elements of Prose Rhythm. Thus far the discussion of language rhythm has been confined to a general perception of rhythmic movement. When an attempt is made to carry the investigation into greater detail, more difficult and from a prosodic point of view really crucial problems present themselves. The essential thing in any perception of rhythm is the experience of groups; but what are the nature and determining qualities of these groups? In music there are bars — the primary rhythmic group, comprising a single rhythmic wave, that is, covering the time-distance from one point of division to another — phrases, cadences, etc. The dual nature of language, however, its union of sound elements and thought elements, gives the question another aspect. Corresponding to the musical bar there is the metrical foot; to the musical phrase, the logical phrase; to the musical cadence, a similar melodious flow of word-sounds. But there are also in prose what are called breath-groups and attention-groups, series of words bound together by the physiological requirements of utterance and the mental requirements of perception and understanding.[1] The first step towards clearness will be a closer distinction between prose and metrical rhythms.

Syllable. The simplest and smallest unit of speech-sound is the syllable; then follow, in increasing magnitude, the word, the phrase (that is, words held together by their meaning or by their sound), the clause, the sentence, the paragraph. These units exist in verse as well as in prose, but while verse has other units (which are arbitrary and artificial), prose rhythm has only these. The rhythm of a paragraph is determined by the length, structure, content, and arrangement of the sentences; that of a sentence by the length, structure,

[1] Compare the sentence from Disraeli on page 24, above.

content, and arrangement of the phrases; that of the phrase by the length, structure, content, and arrangement of the words; that of a word by the character of the syllables. Now syllables, as has been explained above, have the sound attributes of duration, intensity (or lack of intensity), and pitch—called, however, in the terminology of phonetics, length or quantity, accent (or no accent), and pitch. These must be studied individually before their combined effects can be understood.

Length. Length is of course comparative. Some vowels require a longer time to enunciate than others: the *e* in *penal* than the *i* in *pin*, the *o* in *coat* than the *o* in *cot*, etc. Again, some consonants are shorter by nature than others: the explosives *p, t, k*, etc., than the continuants *s, z, th, f, m, n, l*, etc. When vowels and consonants are combined into syllables the comparative length is still more apparent: thus *form* is longer than *god*, *stole* than *poke*, *curl* than *cut*, etc. Moreover, it is not alone the natural quantity of vowels and consonants that affects or determines their length, but also their position in a word and in a sentence. Thus, for example, the same sounds are uttered more rapidly when closely followed by one or more syllables than when alone: as *bit, bitter, bitterly; hard, hardy, hardily.* This elasticity of syllabic quantity is clearly shown in Verrier's examples: [1]

---

[1] Vol. i, pp. 79, 80. The musical notation must be taken as merely approximate.

♩. ♫♩ ♪.♬♪ ♩♪

They come fast — faster yet — faster and faster

♪♩ ♩♪ ♩. ♪♪♬.♪.

Barren mountain tracts — barren affections.

These indications, moreover, cover normal utterance only; in emotional language or elocutionary delivery there are deliberate and arbitrary lengthenings and shortenings.[1]

Accent and Stress. The term *accent* may best be reserved for grammatical or dictionary accent — the greater emphasis placed according to standard usage upon one syllable of a word as compared with the others. Thus *portion* has an accent on the first syllable, *material* on the second, *apprehension* on the third, *deliberation* on the fourth. The other syllables are either unaccented, as the first of *material* and the second of *portion*, or have a secondary accent, as the second of *deliberation*.

Accent should be distinguished from *stress*, which is the rhythmical emphasis in a series of sounds. In prose the rhythmical stress is determined almost wholly by accent; in verse the two sometimes coincide and sometimes differ markedly.

In certain words whose accent is somewhat evenly divided between two syllables, and in certain combina-

---

[1] Experiments have been made to obtain absolute measurements of syllabic quantity, and elaborate rules formulated for determining longs and shorts. Thus far, however, the results have been very variable and unsatisfactory, and should be accepted with great caution.

tions of monosyllables, there is a tendency to subject
even grammatical accent to rhythmical stress. Hence
the common pronunciations *Newfound*land, *Hawthorn*den; the alternation of stress in *poor old man, sad
hurt heart;* and the shift of accent in "In a *Chi*nese
restaurant the waiters are Chi*nese*."

Pitch. Pitch is a very uncertain and variable phenomenon. For the most part it is an ornament or aid
to simple language rhythms, but under some conditions
it plays an important rôle which cannot be neglected.
Because of the physical structure of the vocal organs
pitch is constantly changing in spoken discourse,
though often the changes are not readily perceptible.
Usually it coincides with accent.[1] It is also a frequent
but by no means regular means of intensifying accent:
compare "That was done simply" (normal utterance)
with "That was simply wonderful" (intensive utterance). On the other hand pitch and accent sometimes
clash: compare "The idea is good" (normal utterance)
with "The *i*dea!" (exclamatory). Other examples of

---

[1] To adduce Greek in explanation of English pitch would be a clear
case of *ignotum per ignotius.* But interesting parallels have been noted by
Mr. Stone (in R. Bridges, Milton's Prosody, 2d ed.). "The ordinary un-
emphatic English accent," he says, "is exactly a raising of pitch, and
nothing more" (p. 143); and there are similar habits in English and
Greek of turning the grave accent into acute, as in *to gèt mòney* and *to gèt
it.* The Greeks recognized three degrees of pitch: the acute (high), and
the grave (low), (which, according to Dionysius, differed by about the
musical interval of a fifth), and midway, the circumflex. Compare *thát?*
(acute, expressing surprise); *thât?* (circumflex, expressing doubt); and *thàt
book* (grave — 'book' and not 'table'). The main difference between
the two languages is that so far as we can tell classical Greek had (very
much like modern French) a pitch-accent and very little or no stress-
accent, whereas English has both (though stress-accent preponderates).

pitch as a significant factor in prose are: "One should not say 'good' but 'good*ly*,' not 'brave' but 'brave*ly*'"; "Not praise but prais*ing* gives him delight."[1]

Another aspect of pitch is that which in the rhetorics is usually called inflection. A question is uttered with rising inflection, that is, with a higher pitch at the end. Declarative sentences usually have a falling inflection just before the final period, that is, a lower pitch. Exclamations often have a circumflex inflection, as "Really!" spoken in a sarcastic tone; that is, the pitch rises and falls.

Experimental attempts to indicate variations of pitch by our common musical notation are given by Verrier. A single example will suffice here.[2]

I come from haunts of   coot and   hern

Perhaps the most important aspect of pitch from the point of view of rhythm is its actual influence upon accent. We say naturally: "He was *fif*teen years old"; but place the numeral for emphasis at the end of the sentence and it receives a kind of pitch accent: "His

[1] Cf. J. W. Bright, "Proper Names in Old English Verse," Publications of the Modern Language Association, vol. 14 (1899), pp. 347 ff.; especially pp. 363-365.

[2] Verrier, vol. iii, p. 229. A more ambitious attempt, from Pierson, Métrique naturelle du langage (Paris, 1884), pp. 226, 227, is given by Verrier, vol. ii, p. 14 — a musical transcription of the opening verses of Racine's Athalie.

age was fif*teen*." Compare also *Chi*nese and Chi*nese* in the example above.

Observe carefully the elements of duration, stress, accent, and pitch in the following sentences:

Now he 's a great big man.
He was a *re*markable young fellow, but he had an *un*governable temper.
Off went Joy; on came Despair.

Word and Phrase Rhythm. The next larger unit after the syllable is the word; after the word, the phrase. Something has already been said in the previous paragraphs on word and phrase rhythm: it remains to examine them more closely.

Words vary in length from one to eight or even ten syllables; and the accents (main and secondary) may fall on any of these syllables according to the origin and historical development of the word — thus words of two syllables: *ápple, alóne;* of three syllables: *béautiful, accéssion, appercéive;* of four syllables: *ápoplexy, matérial, evolútion, interreláte.* But generally in polysyllables the tendency to rhythmic alternation of stress produces one or more secondary accents more or less distinctly felt; thus on the first syllable of *apperceive* and on the third of *apoplexy* there is an obvious secondary accent; on the third syllable of *beautiful* and the fourth of *material* there are potential accents, not regularly felt as such but capable, under certain circumstances, of rhythmic stress. For example, in the phrase ' beautiful clothes ' there is no accent and no stress on *-ful*; but in ' beautiful attire ' the syllable *-ful* receives a very slight accent (properly not recognized by the dictionaries) which can well serve as a weak rhythmic stress. Long words illustrate the same principle: *antitranssubstantionalistic, pseudomonocotyledonous, perfectibiliarianism*. This potential stress is of the utmost importance in verse — as when Milton out of three words, two of which have no recognized secondary accent, makes a 5-stress line:

Immutable, immortal, infinite.

Paradise Lost, III, 373.

The result of this tendency to alternation, or in other words of the difficulty of pronouncing more than three consecutive syllables without introducing a secondary accent or stress, is that English phrases fall naturally into four rhythmic patterns or movements (and their combinations): 1. accent + no-accent (*a*. one syllable, *b*. two syllables); 2. no-accent (*a*. one syllable, *b*. two syllables) + accent. Examples: 1a *beauty*, 1b *beautiful*, 2a *relate*, 2b *intercede*. These four movements are variously named: the first two are called *falling*, the second two *rising*; 1a and 2a are called *duple* or *dissyllabic*, 1b and 2b *triple* or *trisyllabic*; 1a is called *trochaic*, 1b *dactylic*, 2a *iambic*, 2b *anapestic* (after the names of the metrical feet in classical prosody). *Beauty*, by this usage, is a trochee, *beautiful* a dactyl, *relate* an iamb, *intercede* an anapest. But these patterns alone are by no means sufficient to explain or register all the phrasal movements of English prose — as a single sentence will show.

He that hath wife and children | hath given hostages | to fortune, | for they are impediments | to great enterprises | either of virtue | or of mischief.   BACON, Essay VIII.

Here the first phrase is in falling rhythm, the second (probably) in rising rhythm, the third is — rising or falling? To some readers it will appear of one sort, to others of another. The fourth phrase is probably rising, the fifth doubtful, the sixth falling, the seventh probably rising. To say that the first phrase is made up of a dactyl and two trochees means very little. The primary fact to be recognized and understood is that these four patterns exist in English speech not as absolute entities but as tendencies. In prose they are discontinuous, irregularly alternating, often hardly perceptible; but they are there as potential forces whose latent effects are brought out by regular metre.

Another problem at once obvious is to determine the limits of a phrase. Some readers will feel "to fortune" in the above sentence as a separate phrase, others will join it to the three words that precede. No rules can be laid down. Two tentative but useful criteria are possible, however. A phrase may be regarded as purely musical, a group of sounds that either by their own nature or by their possibility of utterance in a single expulsion of breath seem to belong together. But this is an uncertain criterion, since we separate the sounds of words with great difficulty from their meaning, and the periods of breathing are subject to arbitrary control. And some phrases are uttered in much less than the time required in normal breathing. The other criterion, sometimes supporting sometimes contradicting the former, is the logical content of words. But this also is uncertain, since logical content ought to hold subject and verb together, whereas in the example

above it clearly does not. And neither breath grouping nor logical grouping will enable us to determine
whether "either of virtue or of mischief" is two phrases
or one.

The limits of the sentence, with its clauses, are,
largely through the modern conventions of printing,
more distinctly felt and observed. But its rhythm is
none the less complex. For it is not only the sum of the
smaller rhythmic movements of word and phrase and
clause, but forms a new entity of itself, created by the
union of the lesser elements — just as a building is
more than its component bricks, stones, and timbers.

Composite Speech Rhythm. Such, briefly described,
are the rhythmic elements of spoken English prose.
When only small sections are analyzed singly, it is possible to understand something, at least, of the intricate
pattern of forces which are interwoven in the rhythms
of ordinary language. When one undertakes to analyze
and express the combined rhythms — musical, logical,
emotional — of connected sentences and paragraphs,
one finds no system of notation adequate; the melodies
and harmonies disappear in the process of being explained. Those who wish to enjoy to the fullest the
rhythmic beauties of English prose must patiently
scrutinize the smallest details, then study the details in
larger and still larger combinations — the balance and
contrast of phrases, the alternation of dependent and
independent clauses, the varieties of long and short
sentences, of simple, compound, periodic sentences —
and finally endeavor to rejoin the parts into a com-

plete whole. To pursue the subject further would be to encroach upon the domain of formal rhetoric and would be out of place here. The best counsel is the old counsel: try to *understand* and *feel* the great passages of the great prose masters. A few examples have been given on pages 25 ff., above; they should be studied diligently.

Prose and Verse Rhythm. It is but a short step from the occasional regularity of rhythm in the passages on pages 27–29 to the deliberately continuous regularity of verse. A tendency to rhythmic flow, it has already been shown, is inherent in ordinary language. When the words are made to convey heightened emotion this tendency is increased, and "the deeper the feeling, the more characteristic and decided the rhythm" (John Stuart Mill). Then, as Coleridge says, "the wheels take fire from the mere rapidity of their motion," and finally we have

> high and passionate thoughts
> To their own music chanted.

Intensified, regularized rhythm is reciprocally both a result of impassioned feeling and a cause of it: hence its double function in poetry. It springs, on the one hand, from "the high spiritual instinct of the human being impelling us to seek unity by harmonious adjustment and thus establishing the principle that *all* the parts of an organized whole must be assimilated to the more *important* and *essential* parts." On the other hand, it "resembles (if the aptness of the simile may excuse its meanness) yeast, worthless or disagreeable by itself, but giving vivacity and spirit to the liquor with which it is proportionally combined." [1]

The question is as old as Aristotle, whether metre, that is, regularized rhythm, is an inalienable and necessary concomitant of poetry. The answer rests on a precise understanding of terms; for the right antithesis, so far as there is one, is not between prose and poetry, but between prose and verse. High and passionate thoughts, true poetical feeling and expression may and do exist in prose, but their most natural and characteristic expression is in verse. The old question has been lately reopened, however, by the anomalous form called ' free-verse.' Only the name is new; the thing itself is, at its best, but a carefully rhythmed prose printed in a new shape: an effort to combine in an effective union some of the characteristics of spatial rhythm with the established temporal rhythms of language. Free-verse will be discussed more fully on a later page; it is mentioned here because it is a natural transition between prose and verse, claiming as it does the freedom of the one and the powers of the other.

[1] Coleridge, Biographia Literaria, ch. xviii. Compare the more poetical expression of the same truth in Carlyle's Heroes, Hero-Worship, and the Heroic in History: "Observe too how all passionate language does of itself become musical — with a finer music than the mere accent; the speech of a man even in zealous anger becomes a chant, a song. All deep things are Song. It seems somehow the very central essence of us, Song; as if all the rest were but wrappings and hulls! The primal element of us; of us, and of all things. The Greeks fabled of Sphere-Harmonies: it was the feeling they had of the inner structure of Nature; that the soul of all her voices and utterances was perfect music. . . . See deep enough, and you see musically; the heart of Nature *being* everywhere music, if you can only reach it." (The Hero as Poet.)

Another means of recognizing the close relations of verse and prose is to try to determine which of several passages of similarly heightened emotion, printed in the same form, was originally verse and which prose.

Yet, as I would not catch your love with a lie, but force you to love me as I am, faulty, imperfect, human, so I would not cheat your inward being with untrue hopes nor confuse pure truth with a legend. This only I have: I am true to my truth, I have not faltered; and my own end, the sudden departure from the virile earth I love so eagerly, once such a sombre matter, now appears nothing beside this weightier, more torturing bereavement.

But follow; let the torrent dance thee down to find him in the valley; let the wild lean-headed eagles yelp alone, and leave the monstrous ledges there to slope, and spill their thousand wreaths of dangling water-smoke, that like a broken purpose waste in air. So waste not thou; but come; for all the vales await thee; azure pillars of the hearth arise to thee; the children call, I thy shepherd pipe.

A late lark twitters from the quiet skies; and from the west, where the sun, his day's work ended, lingers as in content, there falls on the old, gray city an influence luminous and serene, a shining peace. The smoke ascends in a rosy-and-golden haze. The spires shine, and are changed. In the valley shadows rise. The lark sings on. The sun, closing his benediction, sinks, and the darkening air thrills with a sense of the triumphing night — night with her train of stars and her great gift of sleep.

There, suddenly, within that crimson radiance, rose the apparition of a woman's head, and then of a woman's figure. The child it was — grown up to woman's height. Clinging to the horns of the altar, voiceless she stood — sinking, rising, raving, despairing; and behind the volume of incense, that, night and day, streamed upwards from the altar, dimly was seen the fiery font, and the shadow of that dreadful being who should have baptized her with the baptism of death. But by her side was kneeling her better angel, that hid his face with wings; that wept and pleaded for *her*; that prayed when *she* could *not*; that fought with Heaven by tears for *her* deliverance; which also, as he raised his immortal countenance from his wings, I saw, by the glory of his eye, that from Heaven he had won at last.

Dost thou already single me? I thought gyves and the mill had tamed thee. Oh that fortune had brought me to the field where thou art famed to have wrought such wonders with an ass's jaw! I should have forced thee soon wish other arms, or left thy carcass where the ass lay thrown; so had the glory of prowess been recovered to Palestine.

And when, in times made better through your brave decision now, — might but Utopia be! — Rome rife with honest women and strong men, manners reformed, old habits back once more, customs that recognize the standard worth, — the wholesome household rule in force again, husbands once more God's representative, wives like the typical Spouse once more, and Priests no longer men of Belial, with no aim at leading silly women captive, but of rising to such duties as yours now, — then will I set my son at my right hand and tell his father's story to this point.[1]

On the other hand, it is worth observing what effect metrical arrangement has upon the emotional quality and power of words and phrases. Hardly anyone would, perhaps, find the following passages strikingly melodious:

Prince Lucifer uprose on a starr'd night. The fiend, tired of his dark dominion, swung above the rolling ball, part screen'd in cloud, where sinners hugg'd their spectre of repose.

Here there is sweet music that falls softer on the grass than petals from blown roses, or night-dews on still waters in a gleam-

---

[1] The first is from a poem in free-verse, Meditation, by Richard Aldington; the second is blank verse, from the Small Sweet Idyl in Tennyson's Princess; the third is from Henley's Margaritae Sorori (also in free-verse); the fourth is from DeQuincey's English Mail-Coach, Dream Fugue IV (prose); the fifth is from Milton's Samson Agonistes, ll. 1092 ff. (blank verse); the sixth is from Browning's The Ring and the Book, Bk. V (blank verse).

ing pass between walls of shadowy granite; music that lies gentlier on the spirit than tired eyelids upon tired eyes.

But turn these words back to their original metrical order, and it is almost a miracle performed. One recalls Coleridge's definition of poetry as the best words in the best places.

> On a starr'd night Prince Lucifer uprose.
>   Tired of his dark dominion swung the fiend
>   Above the rolling ball in cloud part screen'd,
> Where sinners hugg'd their spectre of repose.
>   MEREDITH, Lucifer in Starlight.

> There is sweet music here that softer falls
> Than petals from blown roses on the grass,
> Or night-dews on still waters between falls
> Of shadowy granite in a gleaming pass,
> Music that gentlier on the spirit lies
> Than tired eyelids upon tired eyes.
>   TENNYSON, Lotos Eaters.

It should now be clear that prose and verse are not so antithetical as is often supposed; that they are only different forms of the same substance, language; two branches from the same root. At certain points they overlap and are practically one; at other points the divergence is obvious but not great; and even in their extreme differences the common basis of the rhythms is the same. In both prose and verse are the same relations of time, stress, and pitch, except that in verse the arrangement and order of them are according to a perceptible pattern. *Verse is but prose fitted over a framework of metre.* Herein lies the whole art of versification, the whole psychology of poetic rhythm, the whole problem of metrical study and investigation.

We must always remember that "a line of verse is a portion of speech-material with all its phonetic features (corresponding to its ethos as well as its logos) *adjusted*, without violence, to a fixed and definite metrical scheme. The two entities, metrical scheme and portion of speech-material adjusted thereto, are distinct and the chief study of the metricist is the manner of adjustment of the latter to the former, the way in which a suitable portion of phonetic liquid is chosen and poured into metrical bottles." [1] Only after having grasped what can be grasped of the subtleties of prose rhythm, and having learned the common forms and patterns of metre, can we put the two together, recognize their new unity, perceive the new rhythmic beauties, harmonies, modulations that spring from their mutual adjustment.

A word may be added here, though the subject is one rather of æsthetics than of prosody, on the function of metre in emphasizing and reinforcing the beauties of thought, emotion, and expression that poetry offers. Two practical illustrations have just been given above. Every writer on poetics, from Aristotle down, has had something to contribute, but the substance of it all may be found in the eighteenth chapter of Coleridge's Biographia Literaria, from which a few sentences have already been quoted.[2] It is not merely that verse by its external appearance notifies the reader, or by its

---

[1] Thomas Rudmose-Brown, "English and French Metric," in Modern Language Review, vol. 8 (1913), p. 104.

[2] A convenient collection of extracts from various writers is made by Professor R. M. Alden in Part IV of his English Verse, New York, 1903.

perceptible regularity notifies the listener, that the writer is putting forth his highest efforts, that language is being driven to its highest possibilities; it is not that the use of verse signalizes greater aims and intentions than the use of prose; but rather that the higher efforts, the greater aims, turn by a natural, spontaneous, but partly mysterious instinct to metrical forms for adequate or fit expression. The poets themselves have proved this. No one, barring a few notable exceptions, who felt the creative powers of poetry within him has dared neglect or refuse the added difficulties and the potential beauties of metre. Not the sense of obstacles overcome, but of possibilities realized prompts to formal rhythms. Music, in Dryden's phrase, is inarticulate poetry; but poetry, while it remains articulate and endeavors to accomplish its own destinies, will always approach as close as its own conditions permit to the powers of music. Some poets are inclined more powerfully to music than others. Burns composed with definite melodies in mind; Shelley often began with a little tune which he gradually crystallized into words; Schiller tells us that inspiration often came to him first in the form of music. Tennyson, Swinburne, and others, have chanted rather than read their poetry aloud. And even Browning, who sometimes appears to prefer discord to music, is found to have studied not only the science of music, but also the musical effectiveness of words.

While it is unquestionably going too far to insist as Hegel does that "metre is the first and only condition absolutely demanded by poetry, yea even more necessary than a figurative picturesque diction"; or even to say that the finest poetry is always metrical; still it remains a simple fundamental truth that metre is the natural form of poetic language. The great exceptions to this — the poetic prose of a Sir Thomas Browne, a Pater, a Carlyle, or the free-verse of Whitman — do but prove its soundness; for we always feel them to be something exceptional, something not quite natural though not quite amiss, something wonderful, like *tours de force*. We would not wish them otherwise, perhaps; but we should doubt them if we did not actually have them before us.

CHAPTER III

METRE

ELEMENTS OF VERSE RHYTHM. The simplest
metrical unit is the syllable; the next higher unit
is the foot, a group of syllables; the next higher unit
the line, a group of feet; then the stanza or strophe.

In some prosodies — as the French and Italian, for
example — the standard unit of verse is the syllable.
The first essential of a line is that it have a certain
number of syllables; the accents or stresses may, theoretically at least, fall anywhere in the line. In English verse also the syllable has sometimes been regarded
as the unit, but for the most part only by a few poets
and prosodists of the late sixteenth, the seventeenth,
and eighteenth centuries.

The foot corresponds in English verse to what has
been described in Chapter I as the rhythmic unit of all
rhythms, namely that which recurs in regular sequence.
It comprises, therefore, a point of emphasis and all
that occupies the time-distance between that point of
emphasis and the following one. In other words, a foot
is a section of speech-rhythm containing a stressed element and an unstressed element, usually one or two
unaccented syllables. So much is clear and undisputed
in theory. But there are few single topics on which
writers on English prosody are so much at variance as

on the further, more accurate definition of the foot. One of the main sources of difficulty, however, is easily removed. The metrical foot is not a natural division of language, like the word or the phrase, but an arbitrary division, like the bar in music, an abstraction having no existence independent of the larger rhythm of which it is a part. The analogy between the metrical foot and the musical bar is very close: they are both artificial sections of rhythm which either in whole or in part may be grouped into such phrases as the ideas or melodies may require.[1] They may be isolated and treated by themselves only for the purposes of analysis, for they are merely theoretical entities, like the chemical elements. There is no reason, therefore, that the foot should correspond with word divisions, no objection to the falling of different syllables of one word into different feet. Thus in Gray's line

> The cur | few tolls | the knell | of part | ing day

both *curfew* and *parting* are divided.[2] Further, the division between clauses may fall in the middle of a foot, as in Wordsworth's lines

> The world | is too | much with | us; late | and soon
> Getting and spending we lay waste our powers.

---

[1] The chief difference perhaps between the foot and the bar is that the latter always begins with a rhythmic stress, whereas the foot may begin with an unstressed element.

[2] Some metrists, holding that every foot should begin with a stress, divide thus:

> The | curfew | tolls the | knell of | parting | day.

Such a division can be justified on several grounds, but it remains awkward and obscures the plain fact of rising rhythm. It does not affect the division of word and foot; for compare Shelley's line:

> Ne | cessi | ty! thou | mother | of the | world.

But another difficulty remains, which is apparent in the second line just quoted from Wordsworth. The general rhythm of the whole sonnet of which these two lines are the beginning is plainly duple rising, or iambic. The first line and the latter part of the second are easily divisible into iambs; but how shall *Getting and spend-* be divided? Clearly *and spend-* is an iamb, but *Getting* is not. Can trochees and iambs occur together in the same line without either obscuring or actually destroying the rhythm? The simpler solution would be to keep the whole line in rising rhythm by regarding *-ing and spend-* as the second foot and ∧ *Gett-* as the first. (The sign ∧ indicates a missing syllable or musical rest. See below, page 63.)

The most common feet are the iamb, the trochee, the anapest, and the dactyl (see above, page 38), to which may be added the spondee. The names are borrowed, not quite felicitously, from classical prosody. Various symbols are in use:

Foot	Symbols			Examples
iamb	∪ ⏤	× ′	*xa*	alone, despair, to walk.
trochee	⏤ ∪	′ ×	*ax*	study, backward, talk to.
anapest	∪ ∪ ⏤	× × ′	*xxa*	interdict, to permit,
dactyl	⏤ ∪ ∪	′ × ×	*axx*	tenderly, after the.
spondee	⏤ ⏤	′ ′	*aa*	stone deaf, broad-browed.

Classical prosody distinguished several other feet, some of which are occasionally mentioned in treatises on English verse: amphibrach ∪ ⏤ ∪, tribrach ∪ ∪ ∪, pyrrhic ∪ ∪, paeon ⏤ ∪ ∪ ∪, choriamb ⏤ ∪ ∪ ⏤.

The objection to the use of these classical terms is not so serious as is frequently supposed. Since Greek and

Latin prosody was primarily quantitative, that is, based upon syllabic length, and every long syllable was theoretically equal to two short syllables, an iamb or ◡ — had the musical value of ♪♩, a trochee of ♩ ♪, a dactyl of ♩ ♪♪, etc. And since no such definite musical valuation can be given to English feet, a Greek iamb and an English iamb are obviously different. But after all there was inevitably an element of stress in the classical feet, and there is a very positive element of time in the English, so that the difference is not so great, and no confusion need result once the facts are recognized. Another set of terms, however, borrowed from the Greek and Latin is open to more grave objection, for no real equivalence exists between the classical and the modern phenomena. The *iambic trimeter* in Greek consists of three dipodies or six iambs; as used by English prosodists it consists of three iambs. The Greek *trochaic tetrameter*, similarly, contains eight trochees, the English 'trochaic tetrameter' but four. The common term *iambic pentameter* is not so objectionable, but is to be rejected because of its similarity to the others, which are actually confusing.

The next larger metrical unit after the foot is the *line* or *verse*. It is distinguished (1) mechanically by the custom of printing, (2) phonetically by the pause usual at the end, and (3) structurally by its use as a unit in forming the stanza. Lines are of one, two, three, or more feet, according to the metrical form used by the poet (see Chapter IV). In rimed verse the end of the line is so emphasized that the line itself stands out as a very perceptible rhythmic unit; in unrimed verse, however, the line is frequently not felt as a unit at all, but is so interwoven with the natural prose rhythm of the words as to be almost indistinguishable to the ear, though of course visible to the eye on the printed page. This fact is easily apparent in reading the second, fifth, and sixth illustrative selections on pages 43, 44.

The *stanza* or *strophe* is a combination of two or more lines of the same or varying lengths, according to a regular pattern chosen by the poet. ' Irregular ' stanzas sometimes occur, in which the thought rhythm is said to control and determine the stanzaic rhythm; that is, the length of line and position of rimes are regulated by the logical and emotional content of the words. On the various kinds of stanzaic structure, see pages 88 ff., below.

Metrical Patterns. It must be fully understood that these metrical patterns of line and stanza are purely formal. They are the bottles into which the poet pours his liquid meaning, or better, the sketched-in squares over which the painter, copying from an old masterpiece, draws and paints his figures. They have no literal or concrete existence. They are no more the music of verse than

is the music of a waltz. They are absolutely fixed and predetermined (though the poet may invent new patterns if he chooses). But he uses them *only as forms* on which he arranges his words and phrases. For the rhythm of language is extremely soft and malleable:

by skilful handling it can be moulded into an infinite variety of shapes. Perhaps the comparison of a stanza by John Donne with a stanza by W. B. Yeats, both based on the same metrical scheme, will help to make this clear. The formal scheme is

$$\cup \underline{} \cup \underline{} \cup \underline{} \cup \underline{} \cup \underline{}$$

> Death, be not proud, though some have callèd thee
> Mighty and dreadful, for thou art not so:
> For those whom thou think'st thou dost overthrow
> Die not, poor Death; nor yet canst thou kill me.
> JOHN DONNE, Death.

> When you are old and gray and full of sleep
> And nodding by the fire, take down this book,
> And slowly read, and dream of the soft look
> Your eyes had once, and of their shadows deep.
> W. B. YEATS, When You are Old.

Even more striking is the difference of rhythmical effect observable in reading, one after the other, a page of Pope's heroic couplets in the Essay on Man, of Keats's same couplets in Endymion, and Browning's same couplets in My Last Duchess.

While the formal pattern remains fixed and inflexible, over its surface may be embroidered variations of almost illimitable subtlety and change; but *always the formal pattern must be visible, audible.* The poet's skill lies largely in preserving a balance of the artistic principles of variety in uniformity and uniformity in variety. Once he lets go the design, he loses his metrical rhythm and writes mere prose. Once we cease to hear and feel the faint regular beating of the metronome we fail to get the enjoyment of sound that it is the proper function of metre to give. On the other

hand, if the mechanical design stands out too plainly,
if the beat of the metronome becomes for an instant
more prominent than the music of the words, then
also the artistic pleasure is gone, for too much uniformity is as deadly to art as too much variety.

> The curfew tolls the knell of parting day,
>   The lowing herd winds slowly o'er the lea,
> The plowman homeward plods his weary way,
>   And leaves the world to darkness and to me.

These verses are regular (as is appropriate for the
theme), and vary comparatively little from the formal
metrical pattern. The coincidence of prose rhythm
and metrical rhythm is almost complete. Yet by
means of small subtleties of variation in pause, word
order, long and short syllables, Gray always saves the
poem from monotony. How far the variations may be
carried, how much the ear may be depended upon for
rhythmic substitution and syncopation, is determined
by many things. Certain lines are unmistakably metrical to all ears and in all positions — such as these
verses of Gray's Elegy. Certain lines are generally felt
to contain daring variations and yet be successful and
effective — such as

> The blue Mediterranean, where he lay.
> > SHELLEY, Ode to the West Wind.

> Myriads of rivulets hurrying thro' the lawn.
> > TENNYSON, Small Sweet Idyl, in The Princess.

Other lines stretch our metrical sense to the breaking
point, and according to individual taste we judge them
bold or too bold — such as Tennyson's

> Take your own time, Annie, take your own time.
>> Enoch Arden.

or Milton's

> Burnt after them to the bottomless pit.
>> Paradise Lost, VI, 866.

In all of these examples the metrical pattern is the same: five consecutive iambs. The modifications illustrate plainly the extraordinary flexibility of language.

Time and Stress. Probably the most disputed point in all prosodic theory is the relative importance of time (duration, syllabic length) and stress (accent) in English verse. Some writers have attempted to explain all the phenomena entirely by stress; others entirely by time. Neither side, of course, has been very successful.[1] The difficulty is partly one of theory and partly one of correct analysis of the facts. Thanks, now, to the attention paid in recent decades by the experimental psychologists to rhythm and metre, we are in a position to reach at least approximate clearness on this vexed point. Since the older theorists have mostly started either from the traditional conceptions of classical prosody or from examination of but a part of the phenomena, their work may be left out of account here. Certainly no great blame attaches to them; they are the Bacons and Harveys and Newtons of metrical science. A more nearly correct analysis of the facts is possible now because with the minutely ac-

[1] An historical survey of the problems and theories, somewhat colored by the author's own theory, may be found in English Metrists, Oxford, 1921, by T. S. Omond.

curate instruments of the scientists to aid us we need no longer trust to the uncertainties of perception and statement of separate individuals. Of course no one today holds the extreme belief that science explains everything; and of course the scientific experiments on the nature and effect of rhythm must have a starting point in the personal equations of those who have submitted themselves to the scientific tests. With all its patience and thoroughness of investigation, experimental psychology is only now establishing itself. But it does offer, on this one mooted point of versification, invaluable help.

The theory presented in the previous pages states that sound rhythm consists of a succession of points of emphasis separated by equal time divisions. This is the ideal rhythm. When subjected to the conditions of metrical language it suffers two alterations. In the first place, our notions of time are extremely untrustworthy. Days vanish in a moment and they drag like years. Very few of us can estimate correctly the passage of five minutes: syllables are uttered in a few hundredths of a second. We are satisfied with the accuracy shown by an orchestra in keeping time; but if we took a metronome to the concert we should find the orchestra very deficient in its sense of time. The fact is that the orchestra knows better than the metronome, that perfectly accurate time intervals become unpleasantly monotonous, that we rebel at ' mechanical ' music. Thus the time divisions of pleasurable rhythm are not mathematically equal, nor even necessarily approximately equal, but are such as are *felt to be equal.*

The second alteration of ideal rhythm is that which results from the conformity of fluid language to its metrical mould. This metrical scheme, based theoretically on equal time units marked by equal stresses, becomes a compromise of uneven stresses and apparently equal time divisions.

Almost every line of verse is a proof of this: both the fact and the explanation are clear when approached from the right angle, and may be tested by carefully prepared statistics. In the following examples the figures beneath each syllable give the time of utterance in tenths and one-hundredths of a second; the figures in parentheses represent pauses.[1] The first, from Paradise Lost, II, 604–614, is in blank verse, with five iambic feet to a line; the second, from Shelley's The Cloud, is apparently irregular, but the basis is clearly anapestic. The ideal rhythm or metrical pattern of the first is

$$\cup \perp \cup \perp \cup \perp \cup \perp \cup \perp$$

regularly repeated. The ideal rhythm of the second is

$$\cup \cup \perp \cup \cup \perp \cup \cup \perp \cup \cup \perp$$
$$\cup \cup \perp \cup \cup \perp (\cup \cup \perp)$$

six times repeated.[2]

[1] I take these figures from the two articles by Professor Ada L. F. Snell in the Publications of the Modern Language Association for September, 1918, pp. 396–408, and September, 1919, pp. 416–435. For the first example I have made an average from the records of three different readers; for the second Miss Snell gives only one set of figures.

[2] The second and fourth lines have two feet each, the alternate lines throughout the rest of the poem have three feet each; but it is noteworthy that the average length of these two short lines (1.61) is only .37 less than the average of the four longer lines (1.98). The first, third, fifth, etc., lines have four feet each.

They fer - ry o - ver this Le - the - an sound
.29   .36   .15 .24   .13   .26   .23   .23   .23   .62   (.18)

Both to and fro,   their sor-row to aug-ment,
.41   .27   .2   .63 (.36) .26   .4   .16 .24   .32   .43   (.6)

And wish and strug-gle,   as they pass,   to reach
.2   .47   .25   .33   .25 (.13) .21   .21   .57 (.4) .24   .35

The tempt-ing stream,   with one small drop   to lose
.14   .32   .3   .69 (.44) .24   .37   .53   .47 (.09) .21 .47

In sweet for - get - ful - ness   all pain and woe,
.2   .37   .19   .28   .17   .25 (.1) .39   .53   .17   .52 (.59)

All in one mo - ment   and so near the brink;
.42   .2   .21   .34   .3 (.47) .27   .28   .37   .11   .57 (.49)

But Fate with - stands,   and, to op - pose the attempt
.23   .39   .28   .66 (.49) .22   .18   .11   .48   .23   .52 (.33)

Me - du - sa with Gor - go - nian ter - ror guards
.15   .33   .15   .21   .3   .3   .23   .28   .21   .51

The ford, and   of it - self the wa - ter flies
.14   .6 (.3) .27   .2   .2   .48   .13   .25   .22   .64

All taste of liv - ing wight,   as once it fled
.26   .48   .16   .19   .18   .43 (.5) .29   .39   .16   .43

The lip of Tan - ta - lus.
.1   .32   .14   .33   .15   .3

I bring fresh showers   for the thirst - ing flowers,
.25   .35   .15   .8 (.15) .15   .15   .3   .2   .6 (.2)

   From the seas and the streams;
   .2   .18   .42   .15   .15   .62   (.75)

I bear light shade for the leaves when laid
.2   .35   .3   .5   .18   .18   .34   .4   .45

   In their noon - day dreams.
   .18   .2   .22   .2   .7   (.6)

From my wings are shak - en the dews that wak - en
.25   .35   .44   .22   .3   .2   .1   .6   .2   .25   .25

   The sweet buds   ev - ery one,
   .1   .35   .53 (.15) .2   .21   .5   (.55)

When rocked to rest   on their moth - er's breast,
.18   .47   .2   .4 (.2) .18   .2   .22   .18   .47 (.4)

   As she danc - es a - bout the sun.
   .2   .2   .45   .2   .1   .25   .2   .5   (.85)

I wield the flail of the lash - ing hail,
.22   .22   .1   .5   .15   .15   .25   .15   .45   (.3)

And whit - en the green plains un - der,
.2 .22 .18 .1 .32 .5 .2 .2 (.5)
And then a - gain I dis - solve in rain,
.22 .38 .1 .55 .15 .2 .7 .15 .55 (.07)
And laugh as I pass in thun - der.
.2 .4 (.2) .15 .18 .39 .18 .22 .25

Two facts emerge from these statistics at once: (1) that in about 90 per cent of the feet the ⏑ or unstressed element is shorter than the ⏊ or stressed element, or, in other words, stress and syllabic length nearly always coincide; and (2) that while there is very great variation in the absolute lengths of short syllables and long syllables, the proportion of average lengths is about 2:4.[1] One need not suppose that the conscious mind always hears or thinks it hears the syllables pronounced with these quantitative proportions. Though we deceive ourselves very readily in the matter of time, it is not true that we have no sense of duration whatever. Quite the contrary. Our cerebral metronome is set when we read verse for about .6 seconds for a foot (.2 seconds for the unstressed element; .4 seconds for the stressed element). If we read faster or more slowly the proportions remain the same. When, however, in Paradise Lost, II, 607,

⏑ ⏊ ⏑ ⏊
with one small drop
.24 .37 .53 .47

[1] This statement is based on Miss Snell's computations from analysis of several records for blank verse and several kinds of lyric verse. The short syllables range in blank verse from .02 to .54, in lyrics from .09 to .7; the long syllables range in blank verse from .08 to .84, in lyrics from .11 to .92. The average length of all long syllables is .4, of all short syllables is .21.

the normal proportions are so patently departed from
that the theoretically unstressed syllable *small* is actually longer than the theoretically stressed syllable
drop, and the foot *small drop* takes 1. second, or $\frac{2}{5}$
longer than the average foot beside it (*with one*, .61
seconds) — when divergences so great as this are both
possible and pleasurable, the conclusion should be, not
that the ear makes no recognition of the time, but that
it is capable, by syncopation and substitution, of ad-
justing itself to a very great possibility of variation
without losing hold of the rhythmic pattern.   Looked
at from one point of view, the extreme variations would
appear to be irregularities and warrant the judgment
that no element of duration exists as a principle of
English verse; but from the right point of view these
variations mean only that the metrical time unit is extraordinarily elastic while still remaining a unit; that
the ear is willing and able to pay very high for the
variety in uniformity which it requires.

Pause. The time element of English verse is affected
also by different kinds of pauses. Three kinds may be
distinguished, two of which belong properly to prose
rhythm as well. (1) The *logical* pause is that cessation
of sound which separates the logical components of
speech. It helps hold together the members of a unit
and separates the units from each other, and never occurs unless a break in the meaning is possible. It is
usually indicated in printed language by punctuation.
(2) The *rhythmical* pause separates the breath groups of
a sentence and therefore concerns language chiefly as a

series of sounds independent for the most part of logical content or symbolism. Though its origin is primarily physiological, it soon induces a psychological state and results in an overuse or overdevelopment of the cerebral metronome. Both readers and writers get into a certain ‘ swing ’ which turns to monotony and singsong in reading and to excessive uniformity of sentence length and structure in writing — what is called a jog-trot style. This pause as it affects the reading of verse is only slightly dependent upon the logical content of words, for it takes its pace, especially in rimed verse, from the normal line length, and tends to make every line sound like every other, regardless of the meaning. (3) *Metrical* pause is primarily independent of the other two, but most frequently falls in with them. It belongs to the formal metrical pattern, and serves usually to mark off the line units. There is thus theoretically a pause at the end of every line, and a greater pause at the end of every stanza. When verses are ‘ run on,’ i. e., when there is no logical pause at the end, many readers omit the metrical pause or reduce it to a minimum. Others, whose rhythmic sense is very keen, preserve it, making it very slight but still perceptible. The metrical pause is greatly emphasized by rime.

There are two other time elements in English verse, related in different ways to each of these three pauses, one which is nearly equivalent to the musical *rest*; the other which is nearly equivalent to the musical *hold*. The latter is common to both verse and prose, and is emotional or elocutionary in origin; "If . . . ," "Well — ?" " *These* roses? ' she drawled." In verse it often coincides with and supports a metrical pause, especially on rime words. Many readers in fact combine the hold and the metrical pause or use them interchangeably. The former, the *rest*, is a pause used to take the place of an unstressed element. As such, however, it does not altogether compensate the break in the normal time-space, but fills in the omission sufficiently to preserve the rhythm of the verse.

These various pauses are all well illustrated in Tennyson's lyric, Break, Break, Break.

> Break, break, break,
> .5 (.6) .5 (.28) .6 (.3)
>   On thy cold grey stones, O sea!
>   .35 .3 .6 .5 .7 (.15) .3 .55 (.65)
> And I would that my tongue could ut - ter
> .2 .2 .4 .2 .25 .4 .18 .18 .3 (.35)
>   The thoughts that a - rise in me.
>   2. .5 .3 .2 .4 .3 .5 (.8)
> O, well for the fish - er - man's boy
> .6 .6 .2 .2 .22 .15 .45 .6 (.55)
>   That he shouts with his sis - ter at play!
>   .2 .18 .55 .25 .2 .35 .18 .2 .6 (.9)
> O, well for the sail - or lad
> .5 (.3) .61 .25 .3 .55 .2 .5 (.45)
>   That he sings in his boat on the bay.
>   .18 .18 .55 .25 .2 .45 .15 .15 .6

Logical pauses occur at the end of ll. 2, 4, 6, 8; and probably after *stones* in l. 2. After *stones* there would be also a rhythmic pause, but it is reinforced and practically replaced by the logical pause. Another rhythmic pause might occur after *tongue* in l. 3, but it is absorbed partly by the length of *tongue* and partly by the necessity of preserving the line rhythm through *utter*. It will be felt, however, if the lines are read thus:

> And I would that my tongue
> Could utter the thoughts
> That arise
> In me.

The metrical pause appears clearly after *utter* in l. 3. The pauses after *boy* (l. 5) and *lad* (l. 7) are both metrical and logical. The hold is illustrated by *O* in l. 5 and l. 7.[1] The rest appears distinctly in l. 1. From reading the whole poem we know that the movement is anapestic. The pattern rhythm for the first line would be

Break   break   break

The number of syllables is three, whereas the other lines have from seven to nine syllables each. That is, before each *break* two light syllables, or their time equivalent, are lacking, their place being supplied by the rest-pause (which is also logical and emotional).[2]

The reader may analyze the comparative lengths of foot, line, pause, and rest in the following record:[3]

[1] In the latter case it is supplemented by a pause in Miss Snell's marking. Many readers would no doubt combine the hold and pause; as was done in fact in l. 5.

[2] It should be noted that the average line length here (including pauses within the line, excluding those at the end of the line) is 2.8, and the first line is therefore only .32 shorter than the average. If additional allowance (omitted in Miss Snell's computation) be made for the theoretical initial ∪ ∪ the average would be 2.85 and l. 1 would total 2.92. If the end pause is included the average would be 3.38 and l. 1 2.78 — a difference of .66; or with the additional allowance the average would be 3.44 and l. 1 3.22. While too much faith is not to be placed in the mere figures, the inference is plain that the rests practically compensate here for the omitted ∪ ∪.

[3] Miss Snell, Pause; a Study of its Nature and its Rhythmical Function in Verse (Ann Arbor, 1918), pp. 78, 79.

Kent - ish Sir Bing   stood for the king,
.4   .32 .46   .8 (.2)   .5   .18 .16   .8 (.6)

Bid - ding the crop - head - ed par - lia - ment swing;
.26   .2   .12   .45   .3   .2   .4   .1   .35   .72 (.6)

And, press - ing a troop   un - ab - le to stoop,
.2   .38   .12 .1   .55 (.2) .18 .26 .12 .2   .58 (.5)

And see the rogues flour - ish   and hon- est folk droop;
.22 .35 .15   .5   .6   .2 (.2) .26 .45 .18 .35 .48 (.75)

Marched then a - long   fif - ty - score strong
.52   .22 .12   .8 (.14) .35 .25   .5   .7   (.7)

Great-heart - ed gent - le - men,   sing - ing this song.
.35   .3   .2 .3   .12   .3 (.45) .44 .25 .28 .68   (.9)

God for King Charles! Pym and such carles
.6 .46 .5   .8 (.5)   .38 .26 .3   .85 (.42)

To the Dev-il that prompts them their treas-on-ous parles!
.18 .18 .35 .25 .42   .5   .38   .2   .38 .1 .32 .75 (.55)

Cav - a - liers, up! Lips from the cup.
.35 .15   .5 (.4) .5 (.4) .6   .3   .12 .4

Pitch. Pitch appears to be sometimes a determining element in rhythm, as has been shown above; but since its chief function in verse is that of supporting the recognized determinants and adding grace-notes to the music, it is omitted here and discussed in Chapter V, below.

Balance of Forces. It is not to be inferred from the foregoing sections that the basis of English metre is time. For the basis of English metre is dual: time and stress are inextricable. Beneath all metrical language runs the invisible current of time, but the surface is marked by stress. The warp of the metrical fabric is time; stress is the woof. And from the surface, of course, only the woof is visible. Moreover, the poet's point of view in composing and generally the reader's

point of view in reading has always been that of the
'stresser.' No poet ever wrote to a metronome accompaniment; extremely few readers are fully conscious — few can be, from the nature of our human
sense of time — of the temporal rhythm that under-
lies verse. Thus it has come about, historically, that
modern English verse is written and regarded as a matter of stress only, because to the superficial view stress
is predominant.[1] Probably the truth is that most poets
compose verse with the ideal metrical scheme definitely in mind and trust (as they well may) to their
rhythmical instinct for the rest. Whatever device they
employ for keeping the pattern always before them,
they do keep it distinctly before them — except perhaps in the simpler measures which run easily in the
ear — and build from it as from a scaffolding. They
may not know and may not need to know that this
metrical scheme does itself involve equal time units as
well as equal stresses. They vary and modulate both
time and stress according to the thought and feeling
the words are asked to express. And though it is a
point on which no one can have a dogmatic opinion,

[1] Modern English verse theory may be dated from Coleridge's famous
manifesto in the prefatory note to Christabel in 1816: "I have only to add
that the metre of Christabel is not, properly speaking, irregular, though it
may seem so from its being founded on a new principle: namely, that of
counting in each line the accents, not the syllables. Though the latter may
vary from seven to twelve, yet in each line the accents will be found to be
only four. Nevertheless, this occasional variation in number of syllables
is not introduced wantonly, or for mere ends of convenience, but in correspondence with some transition in the nature of the imagery or passion." Even here there is implied a vague perception of the time unit, but
Coleridge was apparently unaware of its significance. See Leigh Hunt's
comments in "What is Poetry?" in Imagination and Fancy.

one inclines to the belief that usually the finest adaptations of ideas and words to metre are spontaneous and intuitive. Skill is the result of habit and training, and metrical skill like any other; but there is also the faculty divine. One is suspicious of the

> Laborious Orient ivory sphere in sphere;

for when we can see how the trick is done we lose the true thrill.

It would be absurd to imagine a prosody which was independent of its own materials. It would be absurd therefore not to find in all language the elements out of which verse is made. Indeed, M. Jourdain, having recovered from his first shock on learning that he had actually been talking prose, must prepare for a second: that he has actually been talking potential verse. The three acoustic properties of speech — duration, intensity, pitch — modified by the logical and emotional content of which the sounds are symbolic, combine to produce an incredibly subtle and elastic medium which the poet moulds to his metrical form. In this process of moulding and adjustment, each element, under the poet's deft handling, yields somewhat to the other, the natural rhythm of language and the formal rhythm of metre; and the result is a delicate, exquisite compromise. When we attempt to analyze it, its finer secrets defy us, but the chief fundamental principles we can discover, and their more significant manifestations we can isolate and learn to know. In all the arts there is a point at which technique merges with idea and conceals the heart of its mystery. The greatest poetry is not always clearly dependent upon metrical power, but it is rarely divorced from it. No one would venture to say how much the metre has to do with the beauty of the

> magic casements opening on the foam
> Of perilous seas, in faery lands forlorn.

CHAPTER IV

METRICAL FORMS

1. THE LINE

LINE LENGTH. A line of English verse may contain from one to eight feet. Theoretically, of course, more than eight feet would be possible; but just as there are sounds which the human ear cannot hear and colors which the eye cannot see, so there appears to be a limit beyond which we do not recognize the line as a unit. The most frequently used lines are of four and five feet, most conveniently called, respectively, 4-stress and 5-stress lines;[1] those of one, two, and three feet tend to become jerky, those of more than five to break up into smaller units.

Line Movement. The movement of a line is determined primarily by the foot of which it is composed. It is iambic, trochaic, anapestic, dactylic, according as the metrical pattern is made up of iambs, trochees, etc. Thus

> That time of year thou mayst in me behold
> When yellow leaves, or none, or few, do hang

---

[1] The expression '4-foot line' is too suggestive of fishing or surveying; 'tetrameter' is confusing because of its different usage in classical prosody; '4-stress line' is open to objection because it seems to overlook the temporal quality of the foot. On the whole, however, the last seems preferable.

> Upon those boughs that shake against the cold —
> Bare ruin'd choirs where late the sweet birds sang.
>
> > SHAKESPEARE, Sonnet 73.

is plainly iambic.

> You and I would rather see that angel,
> Painted by the tenderness of Dante,
> Would we not? — than read a fresh Inferno.
>
> You and I will never see that picture.
> While he mused on love and Beatrice,
> While he soften'd o'er his outlined angel,
> In they broke, those "people of importance":
> We and Bice bear the loss forever.
>
> > BROWNING, One Word More.

is plainly trochaic.

> I have found out a gift for my fair,
> I have found where the wood-pigeons breed.
>
> > SHENSTONE, Pastoral Ballad.

is plainly anapestic.

> Take her up tenderly,
> Lift her with care;
> Fashion'd so slenderly,
> Young, and so fair!
>
> > HOOD, Bridge of Sighs.

is plainly dactylic.

But very few poems conform exactly to the metrical pattern. For example, Blake's

> Tiger, tiger, burning bright
> In the forests of the night,
> What immortal hand or eye
> Could frame thy fearful symmetry?

seems clearly to be trochaic; yet the last trochee of each line lacks its unstressed element, and the fourth line has an extra-metrical syllable, *Could*. By itself the fourth line would be called iambic: in this context it is

called trochaic with ' anacrusis,' i. e., with one or
more extra-metrical syllables at the beginning.[1] Or
again in Clough's stanza,

> And not by eastern windows only,
> When daylight comes, comes in the light;
> In front the sun climbs slow, how slowly!
> But westward, look, the land is bright!
> ' Say Not, the Struggle Naught Availeth.'

the movement is clearly iambic, yet the first and third
lines have an extra-metrical syllable at the end. This is
called ' feminine ending.'

Moreover, sometimes the word or phrase rhythm
clashes with the metrical rhythm and makes the resultant seem doubtful. Thus

> Of hand, of foot, of lips, of eye, of brow.
>
> SHAKESPEARE, Sonnet 106.
>
> I slip, I slide, I gloom, I glance.
>
> TENNYSON, The Brook.

are unmistakably iambic, and Wordsworth's

> Pansies, lilies, kingcups, daisies.
>
> To the Small Celandine.

is unmistakably trochaic; but in Tennyson's

> This pretty, puny, weakly little one.
>
> Enoch Arden.
>
> With rosy slender fingers backward drew.
>
> Œnone.

there are metrically five iambs in each line, but also in
each four words that are trochaic. The result is a con-

---

[1] From the point of view of stanzaic rhythm *Could* may be said to
complete the final trochee of the previous line:
> What immortal hand or eye Could
> Frame, etc.

flict of rhythms, a kind of syncopation, which produces a very pleasing variant of the formal rhythm.

Furthermore, in a passage like the following, which everyone recognizes as exquisitely musical, it is not obvious whether the rhythm is iambic or anapestic or trochaic.

> When the hounds of spring are on winter's traces,
>   The mother of months in meadow or plain
> Fills the shadows and windy places
>   With lisp of leaves and ripple of rain;
> And the brown bright nightingale amorous
> Is half assuaged for Itylus,
> For the Thracian ships and the foreign faces,
>   The tongueless vigil, and all the pain.
>
>   SWINBURNE, Atalanta in Calydon.

If the first two syllables be regarded as anacrusis, the first line would be trochaic, with a dactyl substituted for a trochee in the second foot. The third line is apparently trochaic. But only three lines of the eight have a feminine or trochaic ending, and all except the third have iambic or rising rhythm in the first foot; so that it is more simple and natural to consider the last syllable of the first, third, and seventh lines as extrametrical, and call the rhythm iambic-anapestic, or rising. Since the $\cup \perp$ and $\cup \cup \perp$ are both rising rhythm they may be readily substituted one for the other — the appearance of equal time values being preserved — without disturbing the musical flow of sounds. Thus of the thirty-two feet in the eight lines, seventeen are iambs and eleven anapests, two are weak iambs (*-orous*, *-ylus*), one a spondee (*bright night-*), and one monosyllabic with a rest ($\wedge$ *Fills*). Tennyson's Vastness may

also be studied for its combinations of trochees, dactyls, and spondees. Here is one stanza:

Stately purposes, valour in battle, glorious annals of army and
    fleet,
Death for the right cause, death for the wrong cause, trumpets of
    victory, groans of defeat.

Similar combinations, still freer, with frequent anacrusis as well, are characteristic of Swinburne's Hes-
peria; e. g. —

Shrill ⁞ shrieks in our | faces the | blind bland | air that was |
    mute as a | maiden,
  Stung into | storm by the | speed of our | passage, and | deaf
    where we | past;
And our ⁞ spirits too | burn as we | bound, thine | holy but | mine
    heavy | laden,
  As we ⁞ burn with the | fire of our | flight; ah, | love, shall we |
    win at the | last?

The first line of a poem is not always a good criterion
of the metre of the whole poem — though Poe declared that it should be. For Tennyson's The Higher
Pantheism is chiefly in triple falling rhythm, but it
begins

The sun, the moon, the stars, the seas, the hills and the plains.

The first stanza of Campbell's famous Battle of the
Baltic runs:

> Of Nelson and the North,
> Sing the glorious day's renown,
> When to battle fierce came forth
> All the might of Denmark's crown,
> And her arms along the deep proudly shone;
> By each gun the lighted brand,
> In a bold determined hand,
> And the Prince of all the land
> Led them on.

Here the first line might be 3-stress or 2-stress; the second, third, fourth, sixth, seventh, eighth might have three stresses or four; the fifth five or six; the ninth two or one. It is not, in fact, until we reach the

> Again! again! again!

of the fourth stanza that we are sure how the poem ought to be read. But Campbell was not a faultless artist. There is the same metrical ambiguity, however, in Tennyson's

> Come into the garden, Maud,

until the second line shows us we should read it with three stresses, not four. There is a curious verse in Gay's Beggar's Opera which well illustrates the necessity of consulting the context to determine the pattern, for it can, taken by itself, be scanned in three different ways:

> How happy could I be with either.
>
> Air XXXV.

viz., ⌣ ⸍ ⌣ ⸍ ⌣ ⸍ ⌣ ⸍ ⌣ or ⌣ ⸍ ⌣ ⌣ ⌣ ⸍ ⌣ ⸍ ⌣ or ⌣ ⸍ ⌣ ⌣ ⸍ ⌣ ⌣ ⸍ ⌣.

But sometimes it is difficult, if not impossible, to say whether a line or series of lines is in rising or falling rhythm, or what sort of foot is predominant — in other words, what is the formal metrical pattern. This difficulty is, of course, no fault of the poet's: it lies in the complexity of the phenomena, and is after all a weakness of our power of analysis. In the spectrum blue merges into green, red into yellow, and though we invent names for various tints, others still escape classification. And just as some verses combine iambic and anapestic (rising), or dactylic and trochaic (falling) movements, so others combine rising and falling rhythms. For example,

> The mountain sheep are sweeter,
> But the valley sheep are fatter;
> We therefore deemed it meeter
> To carry off the latter.
> > PEACOCK, War-song of Dinas Vawr, from
> > The Misfortunes of Elphin.

This may be trochaic with anacrusis or iambic with feminine endings, but neither quite adequately describes it. Is Shelley's To Night prevailingly iambic or trochaic? All of the twenty-five long lines end with an iamb, but only eleven begin with rising rhythm (thirteen begin with falling or trochaic rhythm, and one is ambiguous). Two of the short lines are definitely iambic, the other eight are doubtful, but apparently trochaic. If it is read as iambic, eleven of the hundred feet in the long lines will be ' irregular '; if it is read as trochaic, eleven likewise will be ' irregular.' Milton's L'Allegro and Il Penseroso contain lines that are purely iambic, as

> And oft, as if her head she bow'd;

some that are purely trochaic, as

> Whilst the landskip round it measures;

and others which are a combination, as

> Bosom'd high in tufted trees.
> Then to the spicy nut-brown ale.
> The melting voice through mazes running.

Again, how shall the following stanza from F. W. H. Myers's Saint Paul be classified?

> Lo, if some strange intelligible thunder
> Sang to the earth the secret of a star,
> Scarce could ye catch, for terror and for wonder,
> Shreds of the story that was peal'd so far.

The metrical scheme appears to be

$$\acute{-}\;\smile\;\smile\;\acute{-}\;\smile\;\acute{-}\;\smile\;\acute{-}\;\smile\;\acute{-}\;\smile$$
$$\acute{-}\;\smile\;\smile\;\acute{-}\;\smile\;\acute{-}\;\smile\;\acute{-}\;\smile\;\acute{-}$$
$$\acute{-}\;\smile\;\smile\;\acute{-}\;\smile\;\acute{-}\;\smile\;\acute{-}\;\smile\;\acute{-}\;\smile$$
$$\acute{-}\;\smile\;\smile\;\acute{-}\;\smile\;\acute{-}\;\smile\;\acute{-}\;\smile\;\acute{-}$$

that is, 5-stress trochaic, with dactylic substitution in the first foot and truncation or catalexis of the last foot in the second and fourth lines; or perhaps iambic, with anapestic substitution in the second foot and a feminine ending in the first and third lines. But when many of these stanzas are read in succession, the movement is found to be

$$\acute{-}\;\smile\;\smile\;\acute{-}\;\smile\;\acute{-}\;\smile\;\smile\;\smile\;\acute{-}\;\smile$$
$$\acute{-}\;\smile\;\smile\;\acute{-}\;\smile\;\acute{-}\;\smile\;\smile\;\smile\;\acute{-}$$
$$\acute{-}\;\smile\;\smile\;\acute{-}\;\smile\;\acute{-}\;\smile\;\smile\;\smile\;\acute{-}\;\smile$$
$$\acute{-}\;\smile\;\smile\;\acute{-}\;\smile\;\smile\;\smile\;\acute{-}\;\smile\;\acute{-}$$

that is, 4-stress falling rhythm, with intermixed duple, triple, and quadruple time.

This introduces a new question, whether English verse admits of a foot resembling the Greek paeon, $-\;\smile\;\smile\;\smile$. The answer seems to be that theoretically it does not, but practically it does.[1] It would, doubtless,

---

[1] Apparent paeons occur now and then, where the usual contraction would reduce them to triple time. Mr. Omond, Study of Metre, pp. 96, 97, gives among others these examples:

> The leaves they were *withering and* sere.
> Our *memories were treacherous and* sere.

POE.

be more accurate to describe the foot as $\perp \cup \breve{\cup} \cup$, for some stress, however slight, is regularly felt on the third syllable. But the poets have had their way, and written what certainly try to be paeonic feet. Thus Macaulay's The Battle of Naseby begins:

> Oh! wherefore come ye forth in triumph from the north,
> With your hands, and your feet, and your raiment all red?
> And wherefore doth your rout send forth a bitter shout?
> And whence be the grapes of the wine-press that ye tread?[1]

And Mr. Kipling's The Last Chantey:

> Thus said the Lord in the vault above the Cherubim,
> Calling to the angels and the souls in their degree:
> "Lo!   Earth has passed away
> On the smoke of Judgment Day.
> That Our word may be established, shall We gather up the sea?"

And Mr. E. A. Robinson's The Valley of the Shadow is in this same rhythm, the first four lines being almost perfectly regular:

> There were faces to remember in the Valley of the Shadow,
> There were faces unregarded, there were faces to forget;
> There were fires of grief and fear that are a few forgotten ashes,
> There were sparks of recognition that are not forgotten yet.

Some have read Browning's A Toccata of Galuppi's to the same tune, but at grave risk of destroying the music.

> The rags of the sail ·
> Are *flickering in* ribbons within the fierce gale.
>
> SHELLEY.
>
> A land that is *lonelier than* ruin.
>
> SWINBURNE.

[1] In the last stanza occurs the foot:

$$\perp \cup \cup \cup \cup$$
she of the seven

Rightly described, this movement is a discontinuous syncopation of fours and twos; the prevailing formal unit is ⏑ ⏑ ⏑, but it is varied now by ⏑ ⏑, and now by simply ⏑, with the usual substitution of ⏑ ⏑ for ⏑. It is an excellent exercise to analyze Jean Ingelow's Like a Laverock in the Lift and observe the pauses, holds, and substitutions. The most notable are ⏑ for ⏑ ⏑ ⏑ (*we too, it's*), and ⏑ (*lass, my love*, l. 5; *thou art mine*, l. 6; *missed the mark*, l. 7, etc.). The third line may be read

> Like a ┆ laverock in the │ lift ∧   etc.

or

> Like a laverock │ in the lift │ etc.

The former seems preferable.[1]

It's we two, it's we two, it's we two for aye,
All the world, and we two, and Heaven be our stay.
Like a laverock in the lift, sing, O bonny bride!
All the world was Adam once, with Eve by his side.

What's the world, my lass, my love! — what can it do?
I am thine, and thou art mine; lift is sweet and new.
If the world have missed the mark, let it stand by,
For we two have gotten leave, and once more we'll try.

Like a laverock in the lift, sing, O bonny bride!
It's we two, it's we two, happy side by side.
Take a kiss from me, thy man; now the song begins:
"All is made afresh for us, and the brave heart wins."

When the darker days come, and no sun will shine,
Thou shalt dry my tears, lass, and I'll dry thine.
It's we two, it's we two, while the world's away.
Sitting by the golden sheaves on our wedding day.

---

[1] See Sidney Lanier's scansion of the first stanza, in his Science of English Verse, p. 228.

How musical and effective this rhythm is, judgments will differ. It is clearly capable of great variety, but the large proportion of light syllables forces heavier stress on some of the accents, and the number of naturally heavy syllables which do not coincide with the metrical stress is excessive; and the almost inevitable result is a thumping which only the deftest manipulation can avoid.[1]

Probably the most striking and successful use of the 4-beat movement is that of Meredith's Love in a Valley. So marked is the time element, with the compensatory lengthenings and pauses, that the poem almost demands to be chanted rather than read; but when well chanted it is peculiarly musical, and when ill read it is horribly ragged and choppy. The whole poem will repay study for the metrical subtleties, but the first stanza is sufficient to illustrate the rhythm (there are normally four $\perp \cup \cup \cup$ in each line).[2]

---

[1] An interesting variation of this rhythm (though perhaps to be related to the Middle English descendant of the Anglo-Saxon long line) occurs in Shelley's Prometheus Unbound, Act I,

> O sister, desolation is a difficult thing.

Compare also Shelley's earlier poem, Stanzas — April, 1814; and for a more recent example:

> Ithaca, Ithaca, the land of my desire!
> I'm home again in Ithaca, beside my own hearth-fire.
> Sweet patient eyes have welcomed me, all tenderness and truth,
> Wherein I see kept sacredly, the visions of our youth.
> AMELIA J. BURR, Ulysses in Ithaca.

[2] This metre has been used, e. g., by George Darley (1795–1846) in The Flower of Beauty (four stanzas) and (rather monotonously) by Charles Swain (1803–74) in Tripping down the Field-Path (cf. Stedman's Victorian Anthology, pp. 17, 76); and more recently by Mr. Alfred Noyes.

Under yonder beech-tree single on the greensward,
　　Couch'd with her arms behind her golden head,
Knees and tresses folded to slip and ripple idly,
　　Lies my young love sleeping in the shade.
Had I the heart to slide an arm beneath her,
　　Press her parting lips as her waist I gather slow,
Waking in amazement she could not but embrace me:
　　Then would she hold me and never let me go?

Examples. There occur examples of 1-, 2-, 3-, 4-, 5-, 6-, 7-, 8-stress iambic, trochaic, anapestic, and dactylic lines, sometimes used continuously and sometimes used in combinations with other lengths. But many of these are unusual, and may be found only by diligent search.[1] Some have already been illustrated in the previous section, others occur here and there throughout this volume, especially in the paragraphs on the stanza; some of the more important, however, are given below. But, of course, the line rhythm is significant mainly as a unit of the longer composition, and brief selections cannot well represent the rhythmic movement of a whole poem. Whenever possible the poem should be read complete.

Attempts have been made to characterize the different feet as slow or rapid, solemn or light, and so on, but they are generally unsuccessful. For though certain measures seem to be inherently unsuitable for dignified themes, or for humorous subjects, there are always contrary instances to be adduced, and it is dangerous to be dogmatic. Anapests are said to be characteristically rapid, hurried, because they crowd more syllables than iambs do into a line; but anapests

---

[1] For a classified collection see Alden, *English Verse*, pp. 24 ff.

are often slow-moving, because there is frequent
iambic substitution and because many important
words — monosyllables, for the most part — have to
do duty for light syllables metrically. Perfect anapests, like perfect dactyls, are comparatively few in
English.

Two-stress and 6-stress anapestic:

> Canst thou say in thine heart
> Thou hast seen with thine eyes
> With what cunning of art
> Thou wast wrought in what wise,
> By what force of what stuff thou wast shapen, and shown on my
> breast to the skies?
>
> SWINBURNE, Hertha.[1]

Three-stress anapestic:

> If you go over desert and mountain,
> Far into the country of Sorrow,
> To-day and to-night and to-morrow,
> And maybe for months and for years;
> You shall come with a heart that is bursting
> For trouble and toiling and thirsting,
> You shall certainly come to the fountain
> At length, — to the Fountain of Tears.
>
> ARTHUR O'SHAUGHNESSY, The Fountain of Tears.

> Though the day of my destiny's over,
> And the star of my fate hath declined,
> Thy soft heart refused to discover
> The faults which so many could find;
> Though thy soul with my grief was acquainted,
> It shrunk not to share it with me,
> And the love which my spirit hath painted
> It never hath found but in *thee*.
>
> BYRON, Stanzas to Augusta.

---

[1] This whole poem abounds in substitutions. See Shelley's The Cloud,
above, pages 59 f., which may be regarded as 2- and 3-stress anapestic
lines, though two 2-stress lines are printed as one.

Four-stress anapestic:

> The Assyrian came down like the wolf on the fold,
> And his cohorts were gleaming in purple and gold;
> And the sheen of their spears was like stars on the sea
> When the blue wave rolls nightly on deep Galilee.
>   BYRON, The Destruction of Sennacherib.

Five-stress anapestic. This is a peculiar metre, usually felt to be choppy and harsh. It has been said that no one can read Browning's Saul and follow both metre and meaning at the same time:

> As I sang, —
>   Oh, our manhood's prime vigour!   No spirit feels waste,
> Not a muscle is stopped in its playing nor sinew unbraced.
> Oh, the wild joys of living! the leaping from rock up to rock,
> The strong rending of boughs from the fir-tree, the cool, silver
>   shock
> Of the plunge in a pool's living water, the hunt of the bear, . . .

Eight-stress anapestic. This is on the whole the longest line possible in English.[1] It is really a *tour de force*.

The trochaic line is generally stiff and thumping. It does not admit of frequent substitutions, for many sub-

---

[1] Tennyson's To Virgil, though it has nine stresses in each line and is therefore an exception to the statement made above, page 69, is shorter in respect of the number of syllables. There is, moreover, a poem, After Death, by Fanny Parnell, consisting of fourteen 10-stress lines. The cumbrousness of the rhythm is apparent in these two specimens — which are rather better than the others —

> Ah, the harpings and the salvos and the shoutings of thy exiled sons re-
>   turning!
> I should hear, though dead and mouldered, and the grave-damps should
>   not chill my bosom's burning.

The whole of this poem may be found in Sir Edward T. Cook's More Literary Recreations, p. 278.

stitutions destroy the trochaic effect. It usually comes
to an abrupt close because feminine endings are not
easy or natural in English. Moreover, there are in the
language so many dissyllabic words of trochaic movement that the resulting frequent coincidence of word
and foot tends to produce monotony. Tennyson once
said that when he wanted to write a poem that would
be popular he wrote in trochaics. Certainly the stresses
are more prominent in trochaic verse than in iambic or
even anapestic; and the untrained ear likes its rhythms
well marked.[1] The Locksley Hall poems are good examples:

Comfort? comfort scorned of devils! this is truth the poet sings,
That a sorrow's crown of sorrow is remembering happier things.
Drug thy memories, lest thou learn it, lest thy heart be put to
    proof,
In the dead, unhappy night, and when the rain is on the roof.

Notable is Tennyson's skill in this 8-stress line in
avoiding the natural break into 4 + 4. This break occurs regularly and is enforced by the rime in Poe's The
Raven. One of the most successful metrically of purely
trochaic poems is Browning's One Word More, a few
lines of which are quoted on page 70.
   Four-stress trochaic.

> Shall I, wasting in despair,
> Die because a woman's fair?
> Or make pale my cheeks with care
> 'Cause another's rosy are?

[1] By a series of experiments C. R. Squire found a natural preference
for duple over triple rhythms (though the triple rhythms seemed 'pleas-
anter '), and for trochaic and dactylic over iambic and anapestic. (Am.
Journal of Psychology, vol. 12 (1901), p. 587.)

Be she fairer than the day,
Or the flow'ry meads in May,
  If she think not well of me,
  What care I how fair she be?
> WITHER, The Author's Resolution.

Souls of Poets dead and gone,
What Elysium have ye known,
Happy field or mossy cavern,
Choicer than the Mermaid Tavern?
> KEATS, Lines on the Mermaid Tavern.

Five-stress trochaic.

Then the music touch'd the gates and died;
Rose again from where it seem'd to fail,
Storm'd in orbs of song, a growing gale;
Till thronging in and in, to where they waited,
As 'twere a hundred-throated nightingale,
The strong tempestuous treble throbbed and palpitated;
Ran into its giddiest whirl of sound,
Caught the sparkles, and in circles,
Purple gauzes, golden hazes, liquid mazes,
Flung the torrent rainbow round.
> TENNYSON, The Vision of Sin.

(Note here the substitutions for special imitative effect.)

Shelley's To a Skylark is in trochaic metre of 3-stress and 6-stress lines.

Dactylic lines are not common except in the imitations of the classical hexameter. Hood's familiar Bridge of Sighs in 2-stress lines, and Tennyson's still more familiar Charge of the Light Brigade (which is, however, only partly dactylic) are good illustrations.

Iambic lines are by very far the most frequent in English verse. No special examples need therefore be given except of the less usual 6-stress and 7-stress lines. On blank verse see pages 133 ff.

The 6-stress line is called the alexandrine (probably from the name of an Old French poem in this metre). It is still the standard line in classical French verse; but the French alexandrine differs from the English, principally in having four stresses instead of six. In English it is usually awkward when used for long stretches, and tends to split into 3 + 3. Lowell called it "the droning old alexandrine." It was employed for several long poems in Middle English; and certain of the Elizabethans tried it: Surrey, Sidney, and Drayton—Drayton's Polyolbion (1613) contains about 15,000 alexandrines. It has not commended itself to modern poets, with one exception, for sustained work. Browning wrote his Fifine at the Fair (1872) in this measure; and while he succeeded in relieving it of some of its monotony, he only demonstrated again its unfitness, in English, for continuous use. A peculiar musical effect is obtained from it, however, by Mr. Siegfried Sassoon in his Picture-Show:

> And still they come and go: and this is all I know —
> That from the gloom I watch an endless picture-show,
> Where wild or listless faces flicker on their way,
> With glad or grievous hearts I'll never understand
> Because Time spins so fast, and they've no time to stay
> Beyond the moment's gesture of a lifted hand.

On the other hand, as the last line of the Spenserian and similar stanzas the alexandrine has proved very melodious and effective, largely by contrast with the shorter lines. A few isolated examples will illustrate some of its powers, but of course the whole stanza should be read together.

And streames of purple bloud new die the verdant fields.
Spenser, Faerie Queen, I, 2, 17.

Which from a sacred fountain welled forth alway.
Ibid., I, 1, 34.

Swinges the scaly horror of his folded tail.
The wakeful trump of doom must thunder through the deep.
With thousand echoes still prolongs each heavenly close.
Milton, On the Morning of Christ's Nativity.

Dart follows dart; lance, lance; loud bellowings speak his woes.
Byron, Childe Harold's Pilgrimage, I, lxxvi.

Where'er the surge may sweep, the tempest's breath prevail.
Ibid., III, ii.

As though a rose should shut, and be a bud again.
Keats, Eve of St. Agnes, xxvii.

Countless and swift as leaves on autumn's tempest shed.
Shelley, Revolt of Islam, I, iv.

Month follow month with woe, and year wake year to sorrow.
Shelley, Adonais, xxi.

With sparkless ashes load an unlamented urn.　　　Ibid., xl.

Our sweetest songs are those that tell of saddest thought.
Shelley, To a Skylark.

The slender stream
Along the cliff to fall and pause and fall did seem.
Tennyson, Lotos Eaters.

Alexandrines were occasionally in the eighteenth century (and more frequently in the late seventeenth) inserted among heroic couplets for variety and special effect, as in Pope's

The huge round stone, resulting with a bound,
Thunders impetuous down, and smokes along the ground.
Odyssey, XI, 737–738.

But Pope himself condemned the 'needless alexandrine '

> That, like a wounded snake, drags its slow length along.
>> Essay on Criticism, 357.

One of the oldest lines of modern English verse is the
so-called septenary (septenarius), having had a nearly
continuous tradition from the twelfth-century Poema
Morale down (in its divided form) to the present. It
began as a single line of seven stresses or fourteen
syllables, and continued to be used as such through the
Elizabethan period, and sporadically even later.[1] But
on account of its customary pause after the fourth
foot, it very early broke into two short lines of four
and three stresses each, and thus the septenary couplet
became the ballad stanza. For example,

> And even the lowly valleys joy to glitter in their sight
> When the unmeasur'd firmament bursts to disclose her light.
>> CHAPMAN, Iliad, VIII.

is essentially the same metre, though printed differently, as

> The western wave was all aflame,
> The day was wellnigh done!
> Almost upon the western wave
> Rested the broad, bright sun.
>> COLERIDGE, Ancient Mariner, Part III.

The more notable long poems in septenaries are
Warner's Albion's England (1586), Golding's translation of Ovid's Metamorphoses (1565, 1567), and Chapman's translation of the Iliad (1598–1611).

---

[1] Wordsworth and Mrs. Browning have written rimed septenaries.

2. The Stanza

Couplet. The line unit is used sometimes singly and continuously, as in blank verse, and sometimes in groups usually held together by rime. These groups are called stanzas or strophes. The simplest stanza is, therefore, the couplet rimed *aa*.[1] Couplets are either unequal or equal in length.

The only much-used unequal couplet is the combination, now old-fashioned, of an alexandrine and a septenary, and called, from the number of syllables, Poulter's Measure, because, says Gascoigne (1575), "it gives xii. for one dozen and xiii. for another." Wyatt and Surrey and Sidney wrote in it; the older drama employed it occasionally; Arthur Brooke's Romeus and Juliet (1562) on which Shakespeare's play was based, is in this measure. The following example is by Nicholas Grimald (1519–62).

What sweet relief the showers to thirsty plants we see,
What dear delight the blooms to bees, my true love is to me!
As fresh and lusty Ver foul Winter doth exceed —
As morning bright, with scarlet sky, doth pass the evening's
    weed —
As mellow pears above the crabs esteemed be —
So doth my love surmount them all, whom yet I hap to see!

---

[1] The usual and most convenient way of indicating stanzaic structure is with small italic letters for the rimes and either superior or inferior numbers for the number of stresses in each line. Thus Landor's Rose Aylmer:

> Ah, what avails the sceptred race!
> Ah, what the form divine!
> What every virtue, every grace!
> Rose Aylmer, all were thine.

is described as $a^4 b^3 a^4 b^3$. The repetition of a whole line is indicated by a capital letter. When all the lines are of the same length, one exponent figure suffices, as $abba^4$ for the In Memoriam stanza.

It survives chiefly in the S.M. (short measure) of the
hymn books and such stanzas as that used by Macaulay in his Horatius:

> From Egypt's bondage come,
>   Where death and darkness reign,
> We seek our new and better home,
>   Where we our rest shall gain.
>
> . . . .
>
> When the goodman mends his armor,
>   And trims his helmet's plume;
> When the goodwife's shuttle merrily
>   Goes flashing through the loom;
> With weeping and with laughter
>   Still is the story told,
> How well Horatius kept the bridge
>   In the brave old days of old.

Other unequal couplets are found in Herrick's A
Thanskgiving to God for his House (a^4a^2) and Browning's Love among the Ruins (a^6a^2).

The equal couplet is used both continuously and,
more rarely except with long lines, as a single stanza.
Sometimes two or three couplets are combined into a
larger stanza. The usual forms of the couplet used
continuously are the 4-stress or short couplet ("octosyllabic") and the 5-stress or heroic couplet ("deca-
syllabic").

Short Couplet. The short couplet in duple iambic-
trochaic movement has proved its worth by its long
history and the variety of its uses. The English borrowed it from the French octosyllabic verse, and employed it chiefly for long narrative poems. Chaucer
used it in his earlier work, the Book of the Duchess,
and the House of Fame; Butler in the serio-comic

Hudibras; Scott, Byron, Wordsworth, and Morris in their Romantic narrative verse. For lyric purposes it was used by Shakespeare and other dramatists, by Milton in L'Allegro and Il Penseroso, and since then by most of the greater and lesser poets. But its effect, especially in long poems, is often monotonous because of the rapid recurrence of the rimes, and its powers are somewhat limited. Except under expert handling it is likely to turn into a dog-trot, and it seems sometimes to lack dignity where dignity is required. On the whole it is better for swift movement, for the obvious reason that the line is short: the frequent repetition of the unit, both line and couplet, produces the effect of hurry.

Never has the short couplet revealed its flexibility to better advantage than in Milton's L'Allegro and Il Penseroso and in Coleridge's Christabel. In Christabel Coleridge believed he was inventing a new prosodic principle, that of counting the stresses rather than the syllables;[1] and though he erred with respect to the originality of his principle, he succeeded in getting a freer movement than the couplet had had since Chaucer. Some of the roughness of Chaucer's short couplets is probably due to the imperfections of our texts, and some also to the haste with which he wrote — it is in this metre that the fatal facility of certain poets has proved the worst bane — but the Chaucerian couplet stands as a prototype (though not literally a model) of the freer flow of Byron's[2] and Morris's

[1] See above, p. 66, n. 1.
[2] Byron follows now one model, now another. In Parisina he consciously tried the metrical scheme of Christabel.

couplets, in contrast to those of Scott and Wordsworth, which resemble the stricter, syllable-counting couplets of Chaucer's friend Gower.

The chief drawbacks of the short couplet, besides monotony, are the tendency to diffuseness of language and looseness of grammatical structure (as in Chaucer and Scott, for instance), and rime-padding, i. e., the insertion of phrases and sometimes even irrelevant ideas, for the sake of the rime.

The chief sources of variety are substitution, pause, run-on lines, and division. The first is very apparent in the much-quoted passage in Christabel:

> The night is chill; the forest bare;
> Is it the wind that moaneth bleak?
> There is not wind enough in the air
> To move away the ringlet curl
> From the lovely lady's cheek —
> There is not wind enough to twirl
> The one red leaf, the last of its clan,
> That dances as often as dance it can,
> Hanging so light, and hanging so high,
> On the topmost twig that looks up at the sky.

The pause offers more difficulties for the poet, and more opportunities; since the line is so short, and the rimes reinforce the regular metrical pause at the end of the line, important grammatical pauses cannot well occur in the middle of the line without danger of breaking the rhythm. The logical pause must, therefore, usually coincide with the metrical and thus emphasize unduly the line unit. Moreover, the quick return of the rime sound causes the couplet itself to be felt as a unit and produces what are called ' closed couplets,' in which the two lines contain an independent idea. To avoid irksome uniformity in this regard three devices are customary: to 'run-on' the meaning from one line to the next, thus momentarily obscuring the metrical pause, to 'run-on' the couplets themselves, and to divide the couplet so that the second verse belongs to a new sentence or independent clause.

> And thus, when they appeared at last,
> And all my bonds aside were cast,
> These heavy walls to me had grown
> A heritage — and all my own!
> 5 And half I felt as they were come
> To tear me from a second home.
> With spiders I had friendship made,
> And watched them in their sullen trade;
> Had seen the mice by moonlight play —
> 10 And why should I feel less than they?
> We were all inmates of one place,
> And I, the monarch of each race,
> Had power to kill; yet, strange to tell!
> In quiet we had learned to dwell.
> 15 My very chains and I grew friends,
> So much a long communion tends
> To make us what we are: — even I
> Regained my freedom with a sigh.
>
> BYRON, The Prisoner of Chillon.

In this passage, which is on the whole conservative and stiff in movement, observe (1) how the pause in the middle of ll. 4, 13, and 17 helps to vary the measure; (2) how many of the verses end with a logical as well as metrical pause; (3) how in ll. 3, 5, 16, and 17 the meaning runs over without pause into the next lines; (4) how the first two couplets and the last two are run together, whereas the third and fourth are both closed and independent; and (5) how at ll. 9 and 10 the couplet is divided. This last device is not very frequent in the practice of any poet except Chaucer; it is well illustrated, however, in these lines from Shelley's With a Guitar to Jane:

> All this it knows; but will not tell
> To those that cannot question well
> The Spirit that inhabits it.
> It talks according to the wit
> Of its companions; and no more . . .

Two other means of varying the swing of the short couplet are to change the order of the rimes (as in the example above from Christabel) or introduce a third riming line (that is, to use triplets with the couplets), and to intermingle shorter lines, as Coleridge does occasionally in Christabel, and Byron at the beginning of The Prisoner of Chillon:

> My hair is gray, but not with years,
> Nor grew it white
> In a single night,
> As men's have grown from sudden fears.

Heroic Couplet. The 5-stress line, both rimed and unrimed, is the most flexible and best adapted to all kinds of subjects that English versification possesses. Its powers range through the tragedy and comedy of Shakespeare, the dignity of the sonnet, and the grandeur of Milton, to the satire of Pope and the informal conversational verse of Mr. Robert Frost. The 4-stress line is too short, the 6-stress is too long (when it does not split into two equal parts); the 5-stress seems to hit the golden average. It is less inclined to ' go ' by itself, and therefore is suitable for slow movements; on the other hand, it is easily divided by pauses and hence is easily relieved of monotony and adjustable to almost all tempos.[1]

The earliest form, historically, of the 5-stress line in English was in rimed couplets; the first poet to use the rimed couplet continuously (as distinguished from occasional use in a stanza) was Chaucer.[2] Blank verse is a modification of the couplet by the simple omission of the rimes at the end.

The history of the heroic couplet may be divided into two periods, that of Chaucer and his followers, Gavin Douglas and Spenser, and that beginning with Marlowe, Chapman, and other Elizabethans and continuing down to the present. This division is peculiar, for it represents a double curve of development, the one comparatively short, the other long. Chaucer's couplet has all the marks of ease and freedom of a fully matured medium: great variety in the pauses, run-on lines and couplets, and divided couplets. (All the means of securing variety for the short couplet, explained above, apply *a fortiori* to the heroic line.) Douglas, in large part, and Spenser pretty fully, adopted and preserved this unfettered movement, though the former anticipates here and there the neat

[1] It is no doubt significant that the rhythmic pulses which come most naturally to us are in twos and threes and their multiples; while even to beat time in fives requires a special effort. In music 5/8 or 5/4 time is extremely rare. There is an example of the latter in Chopin's Sonata I (the larghetto movement).

[2] On the source and origin of the 5-stress couplet in English, authorities are in disagreement. See Alden, English Verse, pp. 177 ff., and the references there given.

balance of the Popian couplet. Then the measure seems to have begun all over again, partly on account of an attack of syllable-counting, with close formal recognition of the line unit and the couplet unit, and gradually worked its way back to its original flexibility.[1]

The following characteristic examples illustrate the chief varieties of the couplet. (Again, they should be supplemented by the reading of longer passages. Pope's couplet, in particular, with its perfection of form according to a few well-marked formulas, reveals its great weakness, monotony, only in the consecutive reading of several pages.)

> Whan that Aprille with his shoures soote
> The drought of Marche hath perced to the roote,
> And bathed every veyne in swich licour,
> Of which vertue engendred is the flour;
> Whan Zephyrus eek with his swete breeth
> Inspired hath in every holt and heeth
> The tendre croppes, and the yonge sonne
> Hath in the Ram his halfe cours y-ronne,
> And smale fowles maken melodye,
> That slepen al the night with open eye,
> So priketh hem nature in here corages;
> Than longen folk to gon on pilgrimages,
> And palmers for to seken straunge strondes,
> To ferne halwes, kouthe in sondry londes;
> And specially, from every shires ende
> Of Engelond, to Caunterbury they wende,
> The holy blisful martir for to seeke,
> That hem hath holpen whan that they were seeke.
>
> CHAUCER, Canterbury Tales, Prologue.

[1] Note Professor Woodberry's praise of the heroic couplet for its simple music, its suppleness, its power of forcing brevity: "the best metrical form which intelligence, as distinct from poetical feeling, can employ." (Makers of Literature, p. 104.)

The Husbandman was meanly well content
Triall to make of his endevourment;
And, home him leading, lent to him the charge
Of all his flocke, with libertie full large,
Giving accompt of th' annuall increce
Both of their lambes, and of their woolly fleece.
Thus is this Ape become a shepheard swaine,
And the false Foxe his dog (God give them paine!)
For ere the yeare have halfe his course out-run,
And doo returne from whence he first begun,
They shall him make an ill accompt of thrift.

SPENSER, Mother Hubberd's Tale.

And in the midst a silver altar stood:
There Hero, sacrificing turtles' blood,
Kneel'd to the ground, veiling her eyelids close;
And modestly they open'd as she rose:
Thence flew Love's arrow with the golden head;
And thus Leander was enamoured.
Stone-still he stood, and evermore he gaz'd,
Till with the fire, that from his countenance blaz'd,
Relenting Hero's gentle heart was strook:
Such force and virtue hath an amorous look.
It lies not in our power to love or hate,
For will in us is over-rul'd by fate.

MARLOWE, Hero and Leander.

But when the far-off isle he touch'd, he went
Up from the blue sea to the continent,
And reach'd the ample cavern of the Queen,
Whom he found within; without seldom seen.
A sun-like fire upon the hearth did flame;
The matter precious, and divine the frame;
Of cedar cleft and incense was the pile,
That breathed an odour round about the isle.
Herself was seated in an inner room,
Whom sweetly sing he heard, and at her loom,
About a curious web, whose yarn she threw
In with a golden shuttle.   A grove grew
In endless spring about her cavern round,
With odorous cypress, pines, and poplars crown'd.

CHAPMAN, Odyssey, V.

Though Chapman sometimes uses the pause and run-on lines freely, the regularity of the foot makes for a certain stiffness and inflexibility.

> She, she is gone; she's gone; when thou know'st this,
> What fragmentary rubbish this world is
> Thou know'st, and that it is not worth a thought;
> He honours it too much that thinks it nought.
> Think then, my soul, that death is but a groom,
> Which brings a taper to the outward room,
> Whence thou spiest first a little glimmering light,
> And after brings it nearer to thy sight;
> For such approaches doth heaven make in death.
>> DONNE, Anatomy of the World.

Donne's metres were notoriously careless — or deliberately irregular. They therefore stand somewhat out of place in the general trend of development.

> O how I long my careless limbs to lay
> Under the plantain's shade, and all the day
> With amorous airs my fancy entertain;
> Invoke the Muses, and improve my vein!
> No passion there in my free breast should move,
> None but the sweet and best of passions, love!
> There while I sing, if gentle Love be by,
> That tunes my lute, and winds the strings so high;
> With the sweet sound of Sacharissa's name,
> I'll make the list'ning savages grow tame.
>> WALLER, Battle of the Summer Islands.

Waller, though his lifetime (1605–87) embraces that of Milton, is the natural precursor of the eighteenth century. His couplets are almost all characteristic of eighteenth-century couplets, which seem to seek perfection within themselves. The aim of Waller, Dryden, Pope, and Johnson was primarily to exalt the couplet and extract from it all its potentialities, not to obscure

it by varied pauses and run-on lines. Waller was
praised by the best critics of his own and the following
generation for the great ' sweetness ' and smoothness
of his verse.

> Of these the false Achitophel was first;
> A name to all succeeding ages curst:
> For close designs and crooked counsels fit;
> Sagacious, bold, and turbulent of wit;
> Restless, unfix'd in principles and place;
> In pow'r unpleas'd, impatient of disgrace:
> A fiery soul which, working out its way,
> Fretted the pigmy body to decay,
> And o'er-informed the tenement of clay.
>
> DRYDEN, Absalom and Achitophel, Part I.

> All human things are subject to decay,
> And, when Fate summons, monarchs must obey.
> This Flecknoe found, who, like Augustus, young
> Was call'd to empire and had govern'd long;
> In prose and verse was own'd, without dispute,
> Through all the realms of Nonsense absolute.
> This aged prince, now flourishing in peace
> And blest with issue of a large increase,
> Worn out with business, did at length debate
> To settle the succession of the State.
>
> DRYDEN, MacFlecknoe.

It is interesting, from a metrical point of view, to compare Chaucer's couplets with Dryden's where he is
translating Chaucer, e. g., in the Knight's Tale and
Palamon and Arcite.

Between 1664 and 1678 it became the fashion, partly
as a reaction against the liberties of the late Elizabethan blank verse, and partly under French influence,
to write drama in heroic couplets. But the undertaking
soon proved abortive.

Others for Language all their care express,
And value books, as women men, for dress;
Their praise is still, — the style is excellent;
The sense, they humbly take upon content.
Words are like leaves; and where they most abound,
Much fruit of sense beneath is rarely found:
False eloquence, like the prismatic glass,
Its gaudy colours spreads on ev'ry place;
The face of nature we no more survey,
All glares alike, without distinction gay:
But true expression, like th' unchanging sun,
Clears and improves whate'er it shines upon;
It gilds all objects, but it alters none.
                              POPE, Essay on Criticism.

Meantime the Grecians in a ring beheld
The coursers bounding o'er the dusty field.
The first who marked them was the Cretan king;
High on a rising ground, above the ring,
The monarch sat: from whence with sure survey
He well observ'd the chief who led the way,
And heard from far his animating cries,
And saw the foremost steed with sharpen'd eyes.
                              POPE, Iliad, XXIII.

Pope's couplets represent the acme of polish and metrical dexterity — a perfect instrument for wit and satire.[1] Thus in the mock-heroic Rape of the Lock these well-modeled couplets prove their mettle, but in the translation of Homer their fatal limitations are easily apparent.

Sweet Auburn! loveliest village of the plain,
Where health and plenty cheered the labouring swain,
Where smiling spring its earliest visit paid,
And parting summer's lingering blooms delayed:
Dear lovely bowers of innocence and ease,

[1] See Pope's own analysis of his system of verse in a letter to Cromwell, November 25, 1710.

Seats of my youth, when every sport could please,
How often have I loiter'd o'er thy green,
Where humble happiness endear'd each scene!
How often have I paus'd on every charm,
The shelter'd cot, the cultivated farm,
The never-failing brook, the busy mill,
The decent church that topt the neighboring hill,
The hawthorn bush, with seats beneath the shade,
For talking age and whispering lovers made. . . .

Ill fares the land to hastening ills a prey,
Where wealth accumulates, and men decay:
Princes and lords may flourish, or may fade;
A breath can make them, as a breath has made:
But a bold peasantry, a country's pride,
When once destroy'd, can never be supplied.

GOLDSMITH, The Deserted Village.

The departure from the petrified couplet was gradual and natural, and influenced greatly by the simpler language and content of the verses. These two specimens show Goldsmith writing in two manners, only a few lines apart. Still freer are Cowper's couplets in his On the Receipt of My Mother's Picture. Byron in English Bards and Scotch Reviewers (1809) and Crabbe in his earlier work, still practised the eighteenth-century couplet (in the Tales of the Hall, 1819, Crabbe varied it to a considerable degree), but the new spirit of the Romantic Movement leavened all the metrical forms, as it did the themes, of poetry. Compare the following examples.

One hope within two wills, one will beneath
Two overshadowing minds, one life, one death,
One heaven, one hell, one immortality,
And one annihilation.

Woe is me!
The winged words on which my soul would pierce
Into the height of Love's rare universe
Are chains of lead around its flight of fire —
I pant, I sink, I tremble, I expire!

Shelley, Epipsychidion.

I rode one evening with Count Maddalo
Upon the bank of land which breaks the flow
Of Adria towards Venice: a bare strand
Of hillocks, heaped from ever-shifting sand,
Matted with thistles and amphibious weeds
Such as from earth's embrace the salt ooze breeds,
Is this; an uninhabited sea-side,
Which the lone fisher, when his nets are dried,
Abandons. . . .   Shelley, Julian and Maddalo.

'Twas far too strange and wonderful for sadness;
Sharpening, by degrees, his appetite
To dive into the deepest.   Dark, nor light,
The region; nor bright, nor sombre wholly,
But mingled up; a gleaming melancholy;
A dusky empire and its diadems;
One faint eternal eventide of gems.
Aye, millions sparkled on a vein of gold,
Along whose track the prince quick footsteps told,
With all its lines abrupt and angular.

Keats, Endymion, II.

Ay, happiness
Awaited me; the way life should be used
Was to acquire, and deeds like you conduced
To teach it by a self-revealment, deemed
Life's very use, so long!   Whatever seemed
Progress to that, was pleasure; aught that stayed
My reaching it — no pleasure.   I have laid
The ladder down; I climb not; still, aloft
The platform stretches!   Blisses strong and soft,
I dared not entertain, elude me; yet
Never of what they promised could I get
A glimpse till now!   Browning, Sordello, III.

> She thanked men, — good! but thanked
> Somehow — I know not how — as if she ranked
> My gift of a nine-hundred-years-old name
> With anybody's gift.   Who'd stoop to blame
> This sort of trifling?   Even had you skill
> In speech — (which I have not) — to make your will
> Quite clear to such an one, and say . . .
>
> BROWNING, My Last Duchess.

> It hath been seen and yet it shall be seen
> That out of tender mouths God's praise hath been
> Made perfect, and with wood and simple string
> He hath played music sweet as shawm-playing
> To please himself with softness of all sound;
> And no small thing but hath been sometime found
> Full sweet of use, and no such humbleness
> But God hath bruised withal the sentences
> And evidence of wise men witnessing;
> No leaf that is so soft a hidden thing
> It never shall get sight of the great sun;
> The strength of ten has been the strength of one,
> And lowliness has waxed imperious.
>
> SWINBURNE, St. Dorothy.

Three-Line Stanza

Stanzas of three lines riming *aaa* (called tercets or triplets) are not very common.   Familiar, however, is Herrick's Upon Julia's Clothes:

> Whenas in silks my Julia goes,
> Then, then, methinks, how sweetly flows
> That liquifaction of her clothes!
>
> Next, when I cast mine eyes, and see
> That brave vibration each way free;
> O how that glittering taketh me!

Other examples are: Threnos (in The Phœnix and the Turtle), Herbert's Trinity Sunday, Quarles' Shortness of Life, Browning's A Toccata of Galuppi's, Tennyson's The Two Voices, Swinburne's After a Reading, and Clear the Way; and (with a simple refrain) Cowper's To Mary:

> The twentieth year is well-nigh past,
> Since first our sky was overcast;
> Ah, would that this might be the last!
> My Mary!

Crashaw's Wishes to his Supposed Mistress rimes $a^2a^3a^4$.

Tennyson's 'O Swallow, Swallow' in The Princess is in unrimed triplets.

On the terza rima see below, page 164.

Four-Line Stanza: Quatrain

The most important quatrains are the ballad stanza, riming $a^4b^3c^4b^3$ or $a^4b^3a^4b^3$ (the Common Measure of the hymnals), with the related Long Measure riming $abab^4$ or $abcb^4$; the In Memoriam stanza $abba^4$; and the elegiac quatrain $abab^5$. These are often combined into 8- and 12-line stanzas, as $abab\ bcbc$ [5] (called the Monk's Tale stanza), $abab\ cdcd$, etc., sometimes with alternating long and short lines. And these, as well as longer stanzas, are frequently varied by the use of repetitions and refrains.[1]

The ballad stanza, with its frequent variations of internal rime and additional verses is excellently illustrated by Coleridge's Ancient Mariner. Similar is Tennyson's Sir Galahad, a 12-line stanza of three

---

[1] For complete lists and examples of all the various stanzaic forms, the larger works of Alden and Schipper should be consulted.

quatrains, $a^4b^3a^4b^3cdc^4d^3efgf^4$. Another common variation is that of Hood's The Dream of Eugene Aram, Wilde's Ballad of Reading Gaol, and Rossetti's Blessed Damozel, $a^4b^3c^4b^3d^4b^3$. The musical roughness of the old ballads should be contrasted with the regularized modern imitations, such as Longfellow's Wreck of the Hesperus. Better imitations are Rossetti's Stratton Water and The King's Tragedy, Robert Buchanan's Judas Iscariot, and W. B. Yeats's Father Gilligan. Sometimes a shorter quatrain is printed as a long couplet and combined into larger stanzas, as in Mr. Alfred Noyes's The Highwayman (which has an additional variation in the inserted fourth and fifth lines):

> The wind was a torrent of darkness among the gusty trees,
> The moon was a ghostly galleon tossed upon cloudy seas,
> The road was a ribbon of moonlight over the purple moor,
> And the highwayman came riding —
>   Riding — riding —
> The highwayman came riding, up to the old inn door.

The variations in Tennyson's The Revenge should be carefully studied.

The ballad stanza is closely similar to the $abab^4$ and $abcb^4$ quatrains, and (as in the Sir Galahad mentioned just above) the two are sometimes united. All three were much used by Wordsworth and many minor poets for lyrics as well as narratives; the result is often an undignified tinkle that takes the popular ear and "makes the judicious grieve." The stanzaic unit is so easily carried in one's mind and so rapidly repeats itself, that there is little opportunity for the necessary pleasing surprises. But that the measure is capable of a simple expressive music is evident from such examples as Wordsworth's 'Lucy' poems. These stanzas, both alone and doubled (as in To Mary in Heaven), were favorites with Burns.

A striking musical effect was obtained by Swinburne in Dolores by shortening the last line of a double quatrain:

> Cold eyelids that hide like a jewel
> Hard eyes that grow soft for an hour;
> The heavy white limbs, and the cruel
> Red mouth like a venomous flower;
> When these are gone by with their glories,
> What shall rest of thee then, what remain,
> O mystic and sombre Dolores,
> Our Lady of Pain.

Similar interesting variations are Coleridge's Love, aba^4b^3 and Wordsworth's The Solitary Reaper.

The In Memoriam stanza ($abba^4$) is named after Tennyson's poem (though that was by no means its first use), because Tennyson gave it a peculiar melody, and, partly for this reason and partly from the length and subject of the poem, almost preëmpted it for elegiac purposes.[1] Characteristic stanzas metrically are these:

> Calm and deep peace in this wide air,
> These leaves that redden to the fall;
> And in my heart, if calm at all,
> If any calm, a calm despair.
>
> And all we met was fair and good,
> And all was good that Time could bring,
> And all the secret of the Spring
> Moved in the chambers of the blood.

---

[1] On its origin and the twenty-five poems in it by seventeen different poets, from Ben Jonson to Clough and Rossetti, before the publication of In Memoriam, see E. P. Morton in Modern Language Notes, 24 (1909), pp. 67 ff.

> Now fades the last long streak of snow,
> Now burgeons every maze of quick
> About the flowering squares, and thick
> By ashen roots the violets blow.

One of the peculiarities of the stanza is the increased emphasis which the rime of the third verse receives from its proximity to that of the second; and this is noticeable both when there is a logical pause after the third verse and when there is none:

> 'Thou makest thine appeal to me:
> I bring to life, I bring to death:
> The spirit does but mean the breath:
> I know no more.' And he, shall he . . .

> I sometimes hold it half a sin
> To put in words the grief I feel;
> For words, like Nature, half reveal
> And half conceal the Soul within.

Run-on stanzas are very frequent; especially remarkable is the periodic movement of the four stanzas of LXXXVI, leading up to the last line —

> A hundred spirits whisper ' Peace.'

"By the rhyme-scheme of the quatrain," says Corson, "the terminal rhyme-emphasis of the stanza is reduced, the second and third verses being the most closely braced by the rhyme. The stanza is thus admirably adapted to the sweet continuity of flow, free from abrupt checks, demanded by the spiritualized sorrow which it bears along. Alternate rhyme would have wrought an entire change in the tone of the poem. To be assured of this, one should read, aloud, of course, all the stanzas whose first and second, or third and fourth,

verses admit of being transposed without affecting the
sense. By such transposition, the rhymes are made alternate, and the concluding rhymes more emphatic.
There are as many as ninety-one such stanzas. . . .
The poem could not have laid hold of so many hearts as
it has, had the rhymes been alternate, even if the
thought-element had been the same." [1] Examples for
this experiment are:

> To-night the winds begin to rise
>   And roar from yonder dropping day:
>   The last read leaf is rolled away,
> The rooks are blown about the skies.   XV, 1.

> I hold it true, whate'er befall;
>   I feel it when I sorrow most;
>   'Tis better to have loved and lost
> Than never to have loved at all.   XXVII, 4.

Compare the slightly different effect of the same
stanza printed as two lines, in Wilde's The Sphinx:

The river-horses in the slime trumpeted when they saw him come
Odorous with Syrian galbanum and smeared with spikenard and
    with thyme.
He came along the river bank like some tall galley argent-sailed,
He strode across the waters, mailed in beauty, and the waters
    sank.

The name 'elegiac stanza' for the *abab*[5] quatrain
comes apparently from its appropriate use by Gray in
the Elegy Written in a Country Churchyard, but it is
not altogether fitting; for it is simply the quatrain
movement of the English sonnet, where no lament is
intended, and it was employed effectively by Dryden
in his Annus Mirabilis, and has been often employed

---

[1] H. Corson, Primer of English Verse, pp. 70 f.

since, without elegiac feeling. For examples see the stanza from Gray, page 55, and the sonnets on pages 129 f. An especially interesting modification is that of Tennyson's Palace of Art, $a^5b^4a^5b^3$.

Five-Line Stanza

Five-line stanzas are formed in various ways, e. g., *aaaba, aabba, aabab, abbba, ababa, ababb*, etc., in lines of three, four, five, etc., stresses.

Six-Line Stanza

Six-line stanzas are formed by similar combinations; the most frequent is the quatrain + couplet, called, from Shakespeare's poem, the Venus and Adonis stanza, *ababcc*[5] (compare the end of the English sonnet and the ottava rima).[1] Familiar examples are Wordsworth's To a Skylark and his fine Laodamia.

> Since thou art dead, lo! here I prophesy:
> Sorrow on love hereafter shall attend:
> It shall be waited on with jealousy,
> Find sweet beginning, but unsavoury end;
>   Ne'er settled equally, but high or low;
>   That all love's pleasure shall not match his woe.
>   Venus and Adonis.

The same rimes with 4-stress verses are also common,[2] for example, Wordsworth's

> I wandered lonely as a cloud
> That floats on high o'er vales and hills,
> When all at once I saw a crowd,

---

[1] Early examples may be conveniently found in the Oxford Book of English Verse, Nos. 75, 96, 102, 108, 172.

[2] For early examples see again the Oxford Book of English Verse, Nos. 74, 140, 182, 184, 187.

A host, of golden daffodils;
Beside the lake, beneath the trees,
Fluttering and dancing in the breeze.

Another important 6-line stanza is the tail-rime or
rime couée, a stanza much used in the Middle English
romances and chosen by Chaucer for his parody, Sir
Thopas. Harry Bailey, mine host of the Canterbury
pilgrims, called it 'doggerel rime.' The simple and
probably normal form is $aa^4b^3cc^4b^3$ or $aa^4b^3aa^4b^3$, which
to save space in the manuscripts was written thus:

Listeth, lordes, in good entent,   Of mirthe and of solas;
And I wol telle verrayment
Al of a knyght was fair and gent   His name was sir Thopas.
In bataille and in tourneyment,

Variations are extremely common: the $aaa^4b^2ccc^4b^2$ of
Wordsworth's To the Daisy, $aaaa^4b^3ccc^4b^3$ of Tennyson's Lady of Shalott, $aa^3b^2ccc^3b^2$ of S. F. Smith's
America, $aaa^3b^2ccc^3b^2$ of Drayton's Agincourt, and the
so-called Burns stanza, in which Burns wrote some
fifty poems, $aaa^4b^2a^4b^2$, e. g., To a Mouse and Address
to the Deil.

Seven-Line Stanza

The most important 7-line stanza is the *rime royale*
or Chaucer (or Troilus) stanza, $ababbcc^5$. In the
Parlement of Foules, the Man of Law's Tale, and
Troilus and Criseyde, Chaucer made it a splendid
vehicle both for narrative and for reflective analysis,
for humor, satire, description, and all the gamut of
emotions; in the fifteenth and sixteenth centuries
James I, Lydgate and Hoccleve, Henryson and Dun-
bar, and Skelton, Hawes and Barclay employed it,

largely in imitation of Chaucer; Wyatt used it in his
Vixi Puellis Nuper Idoneus; and Shakespeare in The
Rape of Lucrece. Since then it has not proved attrac-
tive to the poets — though no reason for its disuse is
obvious — except Wordsworth (in his translations of
Chaucer) and Morris, Chaucer's latest disciple.

> And by the hond ful oft he wolde take
> This Pandarus, and into gardyn lede,
> And swich a feste, and swiche a proces make
> Hym of Criseyde, and of hire wommanhede,
> And of hire beaute, that, withouten drede,
> It was an heven his wordes for to here,
> And thanne he wolde synge in this manere.
>
> Troilus and Criseyde, Bk. III.

> So she, deep-drenched in a sea of care,
> Holds disputation with each thing she views,
> And to herself all sorrow doth compare;
> No object but her passion's strength renews;
> And as one shifts, another straight ensues:
> Sometime her grief is dumb and hath no words;
> Sometime 'tis mad and too much talk affords.
>
> Rape of Lucrece.

> Dreamer of dreams, born out of my due time,
> Why should I strive to set the crooked straight?
> Let it suffice me that my murmuring rhyme
> Beats with light wing against the ivory gate,
> Telling a tale not too importunate
> To those who in the sleepy region stay,
> Lulled by the singer of an empty day.
>
> Morris, Earthly Paradise.

In comparison with the formality of Shakespeare's and
the evenness of Morris's, the ease and smoothness of
Chaucer's stanza are striking. Wyatt's stanzas are
musical in their way.

Eight-Line Stanza

Eight-line stanzas are variously formed — chiefly by the doubling of quatrains, sometimes with different rimes, as *ababcdcd*, sometimes preserving one or another or both rimes, as *ababbcbc*, *abcbdbeb*, *ababacac*, *abababab*, etc. Other varieties are *abcdabcd* (Rossetti) and *aaabcccb* (tail-rime), and *aabbccdd*.

One of the commonest 8-line stanzas is that imported from Italy and called *ottava rima*, *abababcc*. It has been charged with tediousness, and tedious it may become if not sedulously varied. It was introduced, along with so much else from Italy, by Wyatt, and was then employed for different purposes by Sidney, Spenser, Daniel, and others.[1] At the close of the eighteenth century it enjoyed a rebirth. "It had already been used by Harrington, Drayton, Fairfax (in his translation of Tasso's Jerusalem Delivered), and . . . in later times by Gay; and it had even been used by Frere's contemporary, William Tennant; but to Frere belongs the honour of giving it the special characteristics which Byron afterwards popularized in Beppo and Don Juan. . . . Byron, taking up the stanza with equal skill and greater genius, filled it with the vigour of his personality, and made it a measure of his own, which it has ever since been hazardous for inferior poets to attempt."[2] Byron had first adopted the stanza in his translation of Pulci's Morgante Maggiore, which is itself in *ottava rime*. Beppo was written

[1] There are two *ottava rime* in Lycidas, one at the close of the Blind Mouths passage and one at the end of the poem.
[2] A. Dobson, in Ward's English Poets, vol. iv, p. 240.

in 1817, and Don Juan begun in the next year. In 1819 the first four cantos of Don Juan were published; in 1820 Keats published his Isabella, and Shelley wrote his Witch of Atlas, both in the same metre.

Those giant mountains inwardly were moved,
But never made an outward change of place:
Not so the mountain-giants — (as behoved
A more alert and locomotive race),
Hearing a clatter which they disapproved,
They ran straight forward to besiege the place
With a discordant universal yell,
Like house-dogs howling at a dinner-bell.
                    J. H. FRERE, The Monks and the Giants.

To the kind of reader of our sober clime
    This way of writing will appear exotic;
Pulci was sire of the half-serious rhyme,
    Who sang when chivalry was more Quixotic,
And revell'd in the fancies of the time,
    True knights, chaste dames, huge giants, kings despotic,
But all these, save the last, being obsolete,
I chose a modern subject as more meet.
                    BYRON, Don Juan, IV, vi.

A lovely Lady garmented in light
    From her own beauty: deep her eyes as are
Two openings of unfathomable night
    Seen through a temple's cloven roof; her hair
Dark; the dim brain whirls dizzy with delight,
    Picturing her form. Her soft smiles shone afar;
And her low voice was heard like love, and drew
All living things towards this wonder new.
                    SHELLEY, The Witch of Atlas.

Nine-Line Stanza

By far the most important of 9-line stanzas, and one of the finest of all stanzas in English poetry, is the ababbcbc^{5}c^6 invented by Spenser — a double quatrain of

5-stress lines plus an alexandrine. This particular octave had been used by Chaucer in the Canterbury Tales, and is sometimes referred to as the Monk's Tale stanza: the stroke of metrical genius lay in adding the ' supplementary harmony ' of the alexandrine, by which the whole stanza climbs to a majestic close or ebbs in a delightful decrescendo as the poet wills.[1] The long swing of nine verses on three rimes, with the combined effect of the interwoven rimes (*abab* and *bcbc*) united by the couplet in the middle, culminating in the unequal couplet at the close, the extraordinary opportunity of balancing and contrasting the rime sounds, and of almost infinitely varying the pauses — all these render the Spenserian stanza incomparable for nearly every sort of poetic expression.

After the Faerie Queene, the chief poems in this metre are : Shenstone's The Schoolmistress (1742), Thomson's The Castle of Indolence (1748), Burns's

---

[1] On the Spenserian stanza see especially Corson, pp. 87 ff. Lowell's characterization of Spenser's use of it is interesting: "In the alexandrine, the melody of one stanza seems forever longing and feeling forward after that which is to follow. . . . In all this there is soothingness, indeed, but no slumberous monotony; for Spenser was no mere metrist, but a great composer. By the variety of his pauses — now at the close of the first or second foot, now of the third, and again of the fourth — he gives spirit and energy to a measure whose tendency it certainly is to become languorous " (Essay on Spenser). See also Mackail's chapter on Spenser in Springs of Helicon; and Shelley's praise in his Preface to the Revolt of Islam: "I have adopted the stanza of Spenser (a measure inexpressibly beautiful), not because I consider it a finer model of poetical harmony than the blank verse of Shakespeare and Milton, but because in the latter there is no shelter for mediocrity; you must either succeed or fail. This perhaps an aspiring spirit should desire. But I was enticed also by the brilliancy and magnificence of sound which a mind that has been nourished upon musical thoughts can produce by a just and harmonious arrangement of the pauses of this measure."

The Cotter's Saturday Night (1786), Scott's Don
Roderick (1811), Byron's Childe Harold's Pilgrimage
(1818 et seq.), Shelley's Laon and Cythna (The Revolt
of Islam) (1817, 1818), and Adonais (1821), Keats's
Eve of St. Agnes (1820), and the opening of Tennyson's Lotos Eaters (1833).

From the following examples only a limited conception can be gained of the stanza's varied capabilities.
Long passages should be read together — and read, for
this purpose, with more attention to the sound than
to the meaning — in order that the peculiarities of
handling of the different poets may be felt.

> A gentle Knight was pricking on the plaine,
> Ycladd in mightie armes and silver shielde,
> Wherein old dints of deepe woundes did remaine,
> The cruell marks of many a bloody fielde;
> Yet armes till that time did he never wield.
> His angry steede did chide his foming bitt,
> As much disdayning to the curbe to yield:
> Full jolly knight he seemd, and faire did sitt,
> As one for knightly giusts and fierce encounters fitt.
>
> Faerie Queen, I, i, 1.

> With loftie eyes, halfe loth to looke so lowe,
> She thancked them in her disdainefull wise;
> Ne other grace vouchsafed them to showe
> Of Princesse worthy; scarse them bad arise.
> Her Lordes and Ladies all this while devise
> Themselves to setten forth to straungers sight:
> Some frounce their curled heare in courtly guise;
> Some prancke their ruffes; and others trimly dight
> Their gay attyre; each others greater pride does spight.
>
> Ibid., I, iv, 14.

> The whiles some one did chaunt this lovely lay:
> Ah! see, whoso fayre thing doest faine to see,
> In springing flowre the image of thy day.

Ah! see the Virgin Rose, how sweetly shee
Doth first peepe foorth with bashfull modestee,
That fairer seemes the lesse ye see her may.
Lo! see soone after how more bold and free
Her bared bosome she doth broad display;
Lo! see soone after how she fades and falls away.
Faerie Queen, II, xii, 74.

Or like the hell-borne Hydra, which they faine
That great Alcides whilome overthrew,
After that he had labourd long in vaine
To crop his thousand heads, the which still new
Forth budded, and in greater number grew.
Such was the fury of this hellish Beast,
Whilest Calidore him under him downe threw;
Who nathemore his heavy load releast,
But aye, the more he rag'd, the more his powre increast.
Ibid., VI, xii, 32.

O ruthful scene! when from a nook obscure
His little sister did his peril see:
All playful as she sate, she grows demure;
She finds full soon her wonted spirits free,
She meditates a prayer to set him free:
Nor gentle pardon could this dame deny
(If gentle pardons could with dames agree)
To her sad grief that swells in either eye
And wrings her so that all for pity she could die.
SHENSTONE, The Schoolmistress.

And hither Morpheus sent his kindest dreams,
Raising a world of gayer tinct and grace;
O'er which were shadowy cast Elysian gleams,
That played, in waving lights, from place to place,
And shed a roseate smile on nature's face.
Not Titian's pencil e'er could so array,
So fleece with clouds the pure ethereal space;
Ne could it e'er such melting forms display,
As loose on flowery beds all languishingly lay.
JAMES THOMSON, The Castle of Indolence, I, xliv.

The chearfu' supper done, wi' serious face,
They, round the ingle, form a circle wide;
The sire turns o'er, wi' patriarchal grace,
The big ha' -Bible, ance his father's pride:
His bonnet rev'rently is laid aside,
His lyart haffets wearing thin an' bare;
Those strains that once did sweet in Zion glide,
He wales a portion with judicious care;
And ' Let us worship God! ' he says, with solemn air.

                      BURNS, Cotter's Saturday Night.

Now, where the swift Rhone cleaves his way between
Heights which appear as lovers who have parted
In hate, whose mining depths so intervene,
That they can meet no more, though broken-hearted;
Though in their souls, which thus each other thwarted,
Love was the very root of the fond rage
Which blighted their life's bloom, and then departed:
Itself expired, but leaving them an age
Of years all winters, — war within themselves to wage.

             BYRON, Childe Harold's Pilgrimage, III, xciv.

(Childe Harold begins with many deliberate imitations of Spenser's language and style, but soon neglects them. Here perhaps more than in any other metre the tone and subject of the poem determine the movement of the stanza. The above is but one example of Byron's great variety.)

The One remains, the many change and pass;
Heaven's light forever shines, earth's shadows fly;
Life, like a dome of many-colored glass,
Stains the white radiance of eternity,
Until Death tramples it to fragments. — Die,
If thou wouldst be with them that thou dost seek!
Follow where all is fled! — Rome's azure sky,
Flowers, ruins, statues, music, words, are weak
The glory they transfuse with fitting truth to speak.

                   SHELLEY, Adonais, lii.

The ancient Beadsman heard the prelude soft;
And so it chanced, for many a door was wide,
From hurry to and fro. Soon, up aloft,
The silver, snarling trumpets 'gan to chide:
The level chambers, ready with their pride,
Were flowing to receive a thousand guests:
The carvéd angels, ever eager-eyed,
Stared, where upon their head the cornice rests,
With hair blown back, and wings put cross-wise on their breasts.
                                KEATS, Eve of St. Agnes, iv.

During the earlier half of the seventeenth century a small group of poets, imitating Spenser both in substance and in external manner, introduced a number of stanzas, some of them not to be admired, whose chief characteristic is the alexandrine for a last line — e. g., $abababcc^5c^6$, $ababcc^5c^6$, $ababbcc^5c^6$, and $ababbc^5c^6$ (which last is that of Milton's On the Death of a Fair Infant, The Passion, and the introduction to On the Morning of Christ's Nativity). Another modification is that of Milton's Ode itself, $aa^3b^5cc^3b^5d^4d^6$. Matthew Prior attempted to improve the Spenserian stanza in his Ode on the Battle of Ramillies by a rime scheme (suggested perhaps by the English sonnet) $ababcdcde^5e^6$ — of which Dr. Johnson says: "He has altered the stanza of Spenser, as a house is altered by building another house in its place of a different form." Still farther from the Spenserian original, but probably a development from it, is Shelley's To a Skylark $abab^3b^6$ (mainly in falling rhythm); and an extension of this last is Swinburne's Hertha (see above, page 81) $abab^2b^6$ in triple rising rhythm.

Fourteen-Line Stanza: Sonnet

A sonnet is a moment's monument, —
Memorial from the Soul's eternity
To one dead deathless hour. Look that it be,
Whether for lustral rite or dire portent,
Of its own arduous fulness reverent:
Carve it in ivory or in ebony,
As Day or Night may rule, and let Time see
Its flowering crest impearled and orient.
A sonnet is a coin: its face reveals
The soul, — its converse, to what Power 'tis due: —
Whether for tribute to the august appeals
Of Life, or dower in Love's high retinue,
It serve; or, 'mid the dark wharf's cavernous breath,
In Charon's palm it pay the toll to Death.
                              DANTE GABRIEL ROSSETTI.

The sonnet is a world, where feelings caught
In webs of phantasy, combine and fuse
Their kindred elements 'neath mystic dews
Shed from the ether round man's dwelling wrought;
Distilling heart's content, star-fragrance fraught
With influences from breathing fires
Of heaven in everlasting endless gyres
Enfolding and encircling orbs of thought.
                              JOHN ADDINGTON SYMONDS.

A sonnet is a wave of melody:
From heaving waters of the impassioned soul
A billow of tidal music one and whole
Flows, in the "octave"; then, returning free,
Its ebbing surges in the "sestet" roll
Back to the deeps of Life's tumultuous sea.
                              THEODORE WATTS-DUNTON.

It is the pure white diamond Dante brought
To Beatrice; the sapphire Laura wore
When Petrarch cut it sparkling out of thought;
The ruby Shakespeare hewed from his heart's core;

The dark, deep emerald that Rossetti wrought
For his own soul, to wear for evermore.

Eugene Lee-Hamilton.[1]

The only English stanza that can be said to rival the Spenserian in artistic merit is the sonnet: but the two are for very different purposes, the one being nearly always used in long, clearly connected series, generally narrative, the other nearly always as an independent poem. Even when sonnets are written in ' sequences,' the relation of the individual sonnets to each other is rarely very close; the unity of the whole sequence (as in Rossetti's House of Life, for example, or Mrs. Browning's Sonnets from the Portuguese) is one merely of general tone and subject. Some of Shakespeare's sonnets are bound together by an intimate unity like stanzas of one poem; others are completely detached. Occasionally a poem is composed of three or four sonnet-stanzas, as Leigh Hunt's The Fish, the Man, and the Spirit, but even then each sonnet remains an independent whole.

The word ' sonnet,' borrowed with the metrical form from Italy in the late sixteenth century,[2] was at first used loosely for almost any short poem on love not obviously a ' song '; but soon the term became restricted to a poem of fourteen 5-stress iambic lines arranged according to one of two definite rime schemes or their modifications. These two rime schemes are

---

[1] See also the collection of Sonnets on the Sonnet, edited by M. Russell, London and New York, 1898.

[2] On the origin of the sonnet in Italy (Sicily) see the references in Alden's English Verse, p. 267. Still a standard work is C. Tomlinson's The Sonnet, London, 1874.

the original Italian *abba abba cde cde* and the English *abab cdcd efef gg.*

Italian Sonnet. The organization of the subject matter of an Italian sonnet is (at least theoretically) as fixed as that of the rimes. The whole should aim to convey without irrelevant detail a single thought or feeling. The first quatrain, *abba*, should introduce the subject; the second, *abba*, should develop it to a certain point, at which a pause occurs; such is the octave. The sestet continues in the first tercet, *cde*, the thought or feeling in a new direction or from a new point of view, and in the second, *cde*, brings it to a full conclusion.[1] The rime sounds of the octave and those of the sestet should be harmonious but not closely similar.

It stands to reason that very few poets have enslaved themselves to such an imperious master without assuming certain liberties. Very few sonnets of any poetic value can be found conforming strictly to all these requirements. But the general purport of the formal division may be seen in Christina Rossetti's poignant " Remember " —

> Remember me when I am gone away,
>   Gone far away into the silent land;
>   When you no more can hold me by the hand,
> Nor I half turn to go, yet turning stay.

[1] Elaborate rules for the sonnet are given by William Sharp in the introduction to his Sonnets of the Century, and by Mark Pattison in the introduction to his edition of Milton's sonnets. There is valuable matter in the Introduction of J. S. Smart's The Sonnets of Milton, Glasgow, 1921. Compare also the 'divisioni' of Dante's sonnets in the Vita Nuova.

Remember me when no more day by day
  You tell me of our future that you plann'd:
  Only remember me; you understand
It will be late to counsel then or pray.

Yet if you should forget me for a while
  And afterwards remember, do not grieve:
  For if the darkness and corruption leave

  A vestige of the thoughts that once I had,
Better by far you should forget and smile
Than that you should remember and be sad.

The first quatrain says: Remember me when I am gone and we can no longer meet and part as in life. The second quatrain adds: when we can no longer enjoy the companionship of mind, planning what might have been. The sestet continues: Nevertheless, do not let the memory of me become a burden, especially if you ever learn what was in my living thoughts.

Most sonnet writers, while regarding the form as in the abstract something almost sacred, have felt free to mould it in some measure to the immediate demands of their subject — not all, however, with the same success.[1] For the sonnet demands perfection, a single flaw almost cripples it; and few have the absolute command of language necessary to forge a single idea without irrelevance and without omission according to so strict a pattern. Those who are too subservient to the form weaken their poetic thought; those who, like Wordsworth often, are inobedient to the form, produce a poem which is imperfect because it is neither a sonnet

[1] "In the production of a sonnet of triumphant success, heart, head, and hand must be right." Corson, p. 145.

nor not a sonnet. Few have come as near the true balance as Milton at his best. "A hundred Poets," says Sir William Watson,

> A hundred Poets bend proud necks to bear
> This yoke, this bondage. He alone could don
> His badges of subjection with the air
> Of one who puts a king's regalia on.

And yet Milton, while preserving the rime scheme, generally disregards the thought divisions, and in half of his sonnets has the pause, not after the eighth line but within the ninth. Commenting on this division Wordsworth says: "Now it has struck me, that this is not done merely to gratify the ear by variety and freedom of sound, but also to aid in giving that pervading sense of intense unity in which the excellence of the sonnet has always seemed to me mainly to consist. Instead of looking at this composition as a piece of architecture, making a whole out of three parts, I have been much in the habit of preferring the image of an orbicular body — a sphere or dew-drop."

Such a close unity can easily be obtained from the Italian sonnet, as hundreds of examples prove, — Milton's On his Blindness is a striking case, with no full stop until the end of the fourteenth line, — but even better for this object is the rime scheme invented by Spenser and used in a hundred and twenty-one sonnets: *ababbcbccdcdee*. The Spenserian sonnet, however, has found no favor with later poets.

Certain variations in the Italian form are regularly admitted as legitimate. The quatrains must always rime *abba*, but the sestet may rime *cdecde* or *cdcdcd* or *cdedce* or *cdedec*, or almost any arrangement of two or three rimes which does not end in a couplet. And even this last caveat is sometimes disregarded by careful sonneteers. A greater liberty is to vary the rimes of the octave to *abbaacca*. The division of the sestet into two distinct tercets is very rarely maintained; and that of the octave into quatrains is frequently neglected with impunity. Thus the poet adjusts his theme to the strict rules of the sonnet much as he adjusts the natural rhythm of language to the strict forms of metre; the one inescapable requisite being that in neither may he lose hold of the fundamental pattern. But there is this difference, that the sonnet form is extraordinarily firm, and breaks if forced very far from normal. *How* far one may go can be determined only in special cases, for "the mighty masters are a law unto themselves, and the validity of their legislation will be attested and held against all comers by the splendour of an unchallengeable success" (Pattison).

The early Italian sonnets in English, those of Wyatt, Surrey, and Sidney, are very irregular: Sidney's nearly always end in a couplet and rime the octave *abbaabba* or *abababab* or *ababbaba*. Sometimes he uses such a scheme as *ababbababccbcc*. Wyatt has one rimed *abbaaccacddcee*, and Surrey one *ababababababaa*.

Donne's Holy Sonnets (written about 1617, though not printed till 1633, 1635) were regular in form, and were practically the first English sonnets not concerned with love. Milton followed this tradition, and expanded it to further themes — his only successful poems in lighter mood are sonnets — occasional and political subjects —

> . . . in his hand
> The thing became a trumpet, whence he blew
> Soul-animating strains — alas, too few!

On the formal side Milton handled the sonnet, as has been said, with the freedom of a master.

From the time of Milton's (1642–58) very few sonnets were written in England till towards the end of the eighteenth century. Then the form was revived, under the original impulse of the Wartons in the mid-century, by Bowles, and given a new life by Wordsworth and Keats. In 1850 Mrs. Browning published her Sonnets from the Portuguese, and in 1870 and 1881 Rossetti his sonnet-sequence, The House of Life. The latter contains on the whole the truest representatives of the Italian model.

> The soote season, that bud and bloom forth brings,
> With green hath clad the hill and eke the vale:
> The nightingale with feathers new she sings;
> The turtle to her make hath told her tale.
> Summer is come, for every spray now springs:
> The hart hath hung his old head on the pale;
> The buck in brake his winter coat he flings;
> The fishes flete with new repaired scale.
> The adder all her slough away she slings;
> The swift swallow pursueth the flies smale;
> The busy bee her honey now she mings;
> Winter is worn that was the flowers' bale.
> And thus I see among these pleasant things
> Each care decays, and yet my sorrow springs.
>   HENRY HOWARD, EARL OF SURREY.

> With how sad steps, O Moon, thou climb'st the skies!
> How silently, and with how wan a face!
> What, may it be that e'en in heavenly place
> That busy archer his sharp arrows tries!
> Sure, if that long-with-love-acquainted eyes

Can judge of love, thou feel'st a lover's case,
I read it in thy looks; thy languish'd grace,
To me, that feel the like, thy state descries.
Then, e'en of fellowship, O Moon, tell me,
Is constant love deem'd there but want of wit?
Are beauties there as proud as here they be?
Do they above love to be loved, and yet
Those lovers scorn whom that love doth possess?
Do they call virtue there, ungratefulness?

> SIR PHILIP SIDNEY, Astrophel and Stella, xxxi.

Death, be not proud, though some have called thee
Mighty and dreadful, for thou art not so:
For those whom thou think'st thou dost overthrow
Die not, poor Death; nor yet canst thou kill me.
From Rest and Sleep, which but thy picture be,
Much pleasure, then from thee much more must flow;
And soonest our best men with thee do go —
Rest of their bones and souls' delivery!
Thou'rt slave to fate, chance, kings, and desperate men,
And dost with poison, war, and sickness dwell;
And poppy or charms can make us sleep as well
And better than thy stroke. Why swell'st thou then?
One short sleep past, we wake eternally,
And Death shall be no more: Death, thou shalt die!

> JOHN DONNE.

Cyriack, this three-years-day these eyes, though clear
To outward view of blemish or of spot,
Bereft of light, their seeing have forgot;
Not to their idle orbs doth sight appear
Of sun, or moon, or star, throughout the year,
Or man, or woman. Yet I argue not
Against Heav'ns hand or will, nor bate one jot
Or heart or hope; but still bear up, and steer
Right onward. What supports me, dost thou ask?
— The conscience, friend, to have lost them overpli'd
In liberty's defence, my noble task,
Of which all Europe rings from side to side.
This thought might lead me through this world's vain mask,
Content, though blind, had I no better guide. MILTON.

Earth has not anything to show more fair:
Dull would he be of soul who could pass by
A sight so touching in its majesty:
This City now doth like a garment wear
The beauty of the morning; silent, bare,
Ships, towers, domes, theatres, and temples lie
Open unto the fields, and to the sky;
All bright and glittering in the smokeless air.
Never did sun more beautifully steep
In his first splendour valley, rock, or hill;
Ne'er saw I, never felt, a calm so deep!
The river glideth at his own sweet will:
Dear God! the very houses seem asleep;
And all that mighty heart is lying still!

                    WORDSWORTH, Upon Westminster Bridge.

Go from me.   Yet I feel that I shall stand
Henceforward in thy shadow.   Nevermore
Alone upon the threshold of my door
Of individual life shall I command
The uses of my soul, nor lift my hand
Serenely in the sunshine as before,
Without the sense of that which I forbore —
Thy touch upon the palm.   The widest land
Doom takes to part us, leaves thy heart in mine
With pulses that beat double.   What I do
And what I dream include thee, as the wine
Must taste of its own grapes.   And when I sue
God for myself, He hears that name of thine,
And sees within my eyes the tears of two.

                    E. B. BROWNING, Sonnets from the Portuguese.

Of Adam's first wife, Lilith, it is told
(The witch he loved before the gift of Eve),
That, ere the snake's, her sweet tongue could deceive,
And her enchanted hair was the first gold.
And still she sits, young while the earth is old,
And, subtly of herself contemplative,
Draws men to watch the bright web she can weave,
Till heart and body and life are in its hold.
The rose and poppy are her flowers: for where

Is he not found, O Lilith! whom shed scent
And soft-shed kisses and soft sleep shall snare?
Lo! as that youth's eyes burned at thine, so went
Thy spell through him, and left his straight neck bent,
And round his heart one strangling golden hair.

D. G. ROSSETTI, Body's Beauty.

I met a traveler from an antique land,
Who said: Two vast and trunkless legs of stone
Stand in the desert. Near them on the sand,
Half sunk, a shatter'd visage lies, whose frown
And wrinkled lip and sneer of cold command
Tell that its sculptor well those passions read
Which yet survive, stamp'd on these lifeless things,
The hand that mock'd them and the heart that fed;
And on the pedestal these words appear:
"My name is Ozymandias, king of kings:
Look on my works, ye mighty, and despair!"
Nothing beside remains. Round the decay
Of that colossal wreck, boundless and bare,
The lone and level sands stretch far away.

SHELLEY, Ozymandias.

Here the rime scheme is peculiarly irregular, and the result is hardly a sonnet at all. Shelley's manuscript shows that the poem cost him a great deal of trouble.

English Sonnet. Out of the ' irregularities ' and experiments of the early English sonneteers there rapidly developed a new form based on an entirely different principle of division, a series of three quatrains *abab*, *cdcd, efef,* followed by a couplet *gg.* This looser structure, simpler in music and in arrangement of subject matter, soon became a favorite, was used by Surrey and by Sidney, and was adopted by Shakespeare for his hundred and fifty-four sonnets [1] — hence it is

---

[1] Two of these are irregular, the 99th, with fifteen lines (*ababacdcde-fefgg*) and the 126th with twelve (*aabbccddeeff*). Milton's On the Admir-

sometimes called the Shakespearian sonnet. "With this key," said Wordsworth,

Shakespeare unlocked his heart.

But a sonnet in the stricter sense this 14-line stanza of course is not; for it does not aim to possess the balance, contrast, and functional organization of the Italian stanza. It has qualities of its own, however, which give it its own distinction; and, moreover, it is frankly what many sonnets of the stricter form, without the justification of a difficult and definitely organic structure, are: simply a poem of fourteen lines. For many of Wordsworth's and most of Mrs. Browning's sonnets, though they have the rime-scheme of the Italian, have the simple thought arrangement of the English sonnet.

Not many examples are necessary. Some, like the first two below, preserve the metrical division of the quatrains, with the couplet for an epigrammatic summary; others more or less obscure the division.

Combinations of the two sonnet forms not infrequently occur (as in the last example below), but they are not approved by the critics or the theorists, and generally they miss the excellences of both forms, however successful they may be in other respects.

Leave me, O Love, which reachest but to dust,
And thou, my mind, aspire to higher things!
Grow rich in that which never taketh rust:

able Dramatick Poet, W. Shakespear, still traditionally miscalled a sonnet, resembles the latter, with its *aabbccddeeffgghh* or eight couplets. The 16-line stanza of Meredith's Modern Love (*abbacddceffeghhg*) is sometimes loosely called a sonnet.

Whatever fades, but fading pleasure brings.
Draw in thy beams, and humble all thy might
To that sweet yoke where lasting freedoms be;
Which breaks the clouds and opens forth the light
That doth both shine and give us sight to see.
O take fast hold! let that light be thy guide
In this small course which birth draws out to death,
And think how evil becometh him to slide
Who seeketh Heaven, and comes of heavenly breath.
Then farewell, world! thy uttermost I see:
Eternal Love, maintain thy life in me!

SIR PHILIP SIDNEY.

That time of year thou may'st in me behold
When yellow leaves, or none, or few, do hang
Upon those boughs that shake against the cold —
Bare ruined choirs, where late the sweet birds sang.
In me thou see'st the twilight of such day
As after sunset fadeth in the west,
Which by and by black night doth take away,
Death's second self, that seals up all in rest.
In me thou see'st the glowing of such fire
That on the ashes of his youth doth lie,
As the death-bed whereon it must expire,
Consumed with that which it was nourished by.
This thou perceiv'st, which makes thy love more strong
To love that well which thou must leave ere long.

SHAKESPEARE, Sonnet 73.

Poor soul, the centre of my sinful earth,
Pressed by these rebel powers that thee array,
Why dost thou pine within and suffer dearth,
Painting thy outward walls so costly gay?
Why so large cost, having so short a lease,
Dost thou upon thy fading mansion spend?
Shall worms, inheritors of this excess,
Eat up thy charge? Is this thy body's end?
Then, soul, live thou upon thy servant's loss,
And let that pine to aggravate thy store;
Buy terms divine in selling hours of dross;
Within be fed, without be rich no more;

So shalt thou feed on Death, that feeds on men;
And Death once dead, there's no more dying then.

SHAKESPEARE, Sonnet 146.

When, in disgrace with fortune and men's eyes,
I all alone beweep my outcast state,
And trouble deaf heaven with my bootless cries,
And look upon myself, and curse my fate,
Wishing me like to one more rich in hope,
Featured like him, like him with friends possessed,
Desiring this man's art and that man's scope,
With what I most enjoy contented least;
Yet in these thoughts myself almost despising,
Haply I think on thee: and then my state,
Like to the lark at break of day arising
From sullen earth, sings hymns at heaven's gate:
For thy sweet love remembered such wealth brings
That then I scorn to change my state with kings.

SHAKESPEARE, Sonnet 29.

O deep unlovely brooklet, moaning slow
Through moorish fen in utter loneliness!
The partridge cowers beside thy loamy flow
In pulseful tremor, when with sudden press
The huntsman fluskers through the rustled heather.
In March thy sallow buds from vermeil shells
Break satin-tinted, downy as the feather
Of moss-chat, that among the purplish bells
Breasts into fresh new life her three unborn.
The plover hovers o'er thee, uttering clear
And mournful-strange his human cry forlorn.
While wearily, alone, and void of cheer,
Thou guid'st thy nameless waters from the fen,
To sleep unsunned in an untrampled glen.

DAVID GRAY, To a Brooklet.

If I should die, think only this of me:
That there's some corner of a foreign field
That is forever England.   There shall be
In that rich earth a richer dust concealed;
A dust whom England bore, shaped, made aware,
Gave, once, her flowers to love, her ways to roam,

A body of England's, breathing English air,
Washed by the rivers, blest by suns of home.
And think, this heart, all evil shed away,
A pulse in the eternal mind, no less
Gives somewhere back the thoughts by England given;
Her sights and sounds; dreams happy as her day;
And laughter learnt of friends; and gentleness,
In hearts at peace, under an English heaven.

RUPERT BROOKE, The Soldier.[1]

Complex Stanzas: the Ode

Besides the stanzas described above, which are but the most familiar or most important of the great variety of regular English stanzas, there are others which, because they are peculiarly constructed or not regularly repeated, may be called Complex. Such are, for example, the ' trailing vine ' stanzas of Spenser's Prothalamion ($abba^5a^3bcbc^5c^3dded^5ee^3ff^5$) and Epithalamion ($ababc^5c^3dcde^5e^3fggf^5f^4hh^5$), and also the simpler $ababcde^5c^3de^5$ of Keats' Ode to a Nightingale.

Many of these complex stanzaic forms, moreover, belong in the tradition of the so-called Pindaric ode, imitated freely from the Greek choric odes of Pindar. The closer imitations are in fixed though complex stanzas regularly repeated, and are called Regular Pindarics. These have first a strophe of undetermined length, then an antistrophe identical in structure with the strophe, and then an epode, different in structure from the strophe and antistrophe. The second strophe and second antistrophe are identical metrically with the first, the second epode with the first epode; and so on. The best examples in English are Ben Jonson's On

[1] Quoted by permission of Dodd, Mead & Co., owners of the copyright.

the Death of Sir H. Morrison, and Gray's Progress of Poesy and The Bard.[1]

About the middle of the seventeenth century, Cowley, misunderstanding the structure of Pindar's verse, invented another sort of Pindaric ode, which is called Irregular because, as he himself explained, "the numbers are various and irregular," and there was no formal stanzaic repetition. The lines were long or short according as the thought-rhythm demanded (or seemed to demand), and in respect to arrangement were not bound to any formal pattern. This freedom, under skilful control, may well produce felicitous results, but when not managed by poets of a strong and sure rhythmic sense — as it was not by the many Cowleyan imitators — it results merely in metrical license and amorphousness. "That for which I think this inequality of number is chiefly to be preferred," said Dr. Sprat, the first historian of the Royal Society, intending no sarcasm, "is its affinity with prose." But this argument, which is in part also that of the modern free-versifiers, is simply a confusion of two functions, the verse function and the prose function.

But before very long Cowley's invention found a true master in Dryden, whose To the Pious Memory of . . Mrs. Anne Killigrew (1686), Song for St. Cecelia's Day (1687), and Alexander's Feast (1697) are justly praised for their ' concerted music.' The example had in fact already been set by a still greater master; for Milton

[1] The rime scheme of the Progress of Poesy is: strophe and antistrophe $a^4b^5b^4a^5cc^4d^5d^4e^5e^4f^4f^6$, epode $aabb^4a^3ccdede^4fgfgh^5h^6$. The formula is three times repeated. Note the unusual arrangement of parts in Collins' Ode to Liberty and Shelley's Ode to Naples.

with his early experiments in unequal rimed lines (On Time and At a Solemn Music), his incomparable success with the irregular placing of rimes in Lycidas, and his choral effects both with and without rime in Samson Agonistes, had shown what English could do under proper guidance. Then, after Dryden, the regular Pindarics of Gray and certain of Collins' Odes helped to carry on the tradition down to Coleridge's Dejection, Monody on the Death of Chatterton, and Ode on the Departing Year, and its culmination in Wordsworth's Intimations of Immortality ode (1807). After that, both in time and in interest, come Shelley's Mont Blanc (1816) (which he himself described as "an undisciplined overflowing of the soul") and Tennyson's On the Death of the Duke of Wellington (1852) (which has at least Tennyson's almost unfailing technical dexterity). The work of Coventry Patmore in this kind of verse has not been generally approved. This is partly because of the subjects on which he wrote and partly because of his inability to compose lines of haunting melody — perhaps his deliberate avoidance of them. But in certain poems like The Azalea and The Toys the very intensity of the feeling both creates and sustains and in the end justifies the ' irregular ' metre.

3. BLANK VERSE

Perhaps three-fourths of the greatest English poetry is in the unrimed 5-stress line called blank verse — nearly all the Elizabethan drama, Paradise Lost, some of the best of Keats and Shelley, Wordsworth's Michael, The Prelude, The Excursion (the good with the bad!), Tennyson's Princess and Idylls (notable poems of their age, though not to be ranked with ' the greatest '), and Browning's The Ring and the Book, together with most of the dramatic monologues. No other metrical form has such an interesting history; no other form has manifested so great a variety and adaptability for every kind of poetic thought and feeling. These two facts alone—its bulk and its variety—would justify a much fuller treatment than is possible here. But it will perhaps be sufficient to follow rapidly in outline the development of blank verse, with illustrations of the most significant stages, and then, in the following chapter, to devote more attention to blank verse than to rimed stanzas in the exposition of metrical harmonies and modulations.

The idea of writing unrimed verse was no doubt the most valuable result to English poetry of the academic attempts, towards the end of the sixteenth century, to write classical verse in English. It could be pointed out triumphantly that all the splendid poetry of classical antiquity — Homer and Lucretius and Virgil, Sappho and Catullus and Horace and Ovid — had been independent of rime; and whatever might be the disagreement on quantitative feet in English, it was impossible to deny that English could successfully copy this element of the great classical verse and recover, as Milton said, the ancient liberty "from the troublesome and modern bondage of riming."

The movement had already begun in Italy with Trissino's Sophonisbe, written in 1515, the first modern tragedy. It reached England in the middle of the

century with the influence of the Italian Renaissance
brought chiefly by Wyatt and Surrey. Surrey trans-
lated two books of the Æneid (II and IV) into blank
verse (published in 1557); Sackville and Norton
adopted it for the first English tragedy, Gorboduc
(1565); and then Gascoigne used it in his Steele Glas
(1576) for general didactic and satiric purposes. Thus
the beginning was made, and it remained only for the
new form to justify itself by its children. Experiments
continued, with the first great achievement in Marlowe's Tamburlaine the Great.

The early examples show plainly both the influence
of the parent couplet — for, as was said above, blank
verse was written first as the old couplet without rime
— and the syllable-counting principle: the line unit is
prominent, there are comparatively few run-on lines or
couplets, and some of Surrey's verse, for example,
though it has the ten syllables then regarded as necessary, refuses to ' scan ' according to more recent practice because the stresses are wholly irregular. On the
other hand, there is often so great a regularity in coincidence of natural rhythm and metrical pattern, reinforced by some awkward wrenches of the conventional
order of word and phrase, that the result is unpleasantly stiff and formal.

> The Greeks' chieftains all irked with the war
> Wherein they wasted had so many years,
> And oft repuls'd by fatal destiny,
> A huge horse made, high raised like a hill,
> By the divine science of Minerva:
> Of cloven fir compacted were his ribs;
> For their return a feigned sacrifice:
> The fame whereof so wander'd it at point.

In the dark bulk they clos'd bodies of men
Chosen by lot, and did enstuff by stealth
The hollow womb with armed soldiers.
    There stands in sight an isle, high Tenedon,
Rich, and of fame, while Priam's kingdom stood;
Now but a bay, and road, unsure for ship.
                    SURREY, Second Book of Virgil's Æneid.

This is not so much monotonously regular as intolerably rough and unsteady.

For cares of kings, that rule as you have rul'd,
For public wealth, and not for private joy,
Do waste man's life and hasten crooked age,
With furrowed face, and with enfeebled limbs,
To draw on creeping death a swifter pace.
They two, yet young, shall bear the parted reign
With greater ease than one, now old, alone
Can wield the whole, for whom much harder is
With lessened strength the double weight to bear.
                    Gorboduc, Act I, sc. ii.

The Nightingale, whose happy noble hart,
No dole can daunt, nor fearful force affright,
Whose chereful voice, doth comfort saddest wights,
When she hir self, hath little cause to sing,
Whom lovers love, bicause she plaines their greves,
She wraies their woes, and yet relieves their payne,
Whom worthy mindes, always esteemed much,
And gravest yeares, have not disdainde hir notes:
(Only that king proud Tereus by his name
With murdring knife, did carve hir pleasant tong,
To cover so, his own foule filthy fault)
This worthy bird, hath taught my weary Muze,
To sing a song, in spight of their despight,
Which work my woe, withouten cause or crime . . .
                    The Steele Glas.

Note here the monotonous pauses, indicated by the original punctuation.

Marlowe, inheriting the defects of his predecessors,

succeeded, by virtue of his "plastic energy and power of harmonious modulation" in recreating the measure. He found it "monotonous, monosyllabic, and divided into five feet of tolerably regular alternate short and long [i. e., unstressed and stressed]. He left it various in form and structure, sometimes redundant by a syllable, sometimes deficient, enriched with unexpected emphases and changes in the beat. He found no sequence or attempt at periods; one line succeeded another with insipid regularity, and all were made after the same model. He grouped his verse according to the sense, obeying an internal law of melody, and allowing the thought contained in his words to dominate their form. He did not force his metre to preserve a fixed and unalterable type, but suffered it to assume most variable modulations, the whole beauty of which depended upon their perfect adaptation to the current of his ideal." [1] No metre responds so readily and so completely to a poet's endowment of genius as blank verse, and hence the secret of Marlowe's improvements over his predecessors is his superior poetic gift. He seems to have felt and thought and written with an enormous imaginative power; by making his verse an organic expression of this power he achieved an almost new medium, ranging in variety from the simplicity and pathos of —

> Mortimer! who talks of Mortimer,
> Who wounds me with the name of Mortimer,
> That bloody man?

[1] J. A. Symonds, Blank Verse, London, 1895, p. 23. (This little volume contains a valuable, though incomplete and somewhat extravagant, summary of the history of English blank verse.)

to the "swelling bombast of bragging blank verse"
(Thomas Nash's hostile phrase) in Tamburlaine —

> No! for I shall not die.
> See, where my slave, the ugly monster, Death,
> Shaking and quivering, pale and wan for fear,
> Stands aiming at me with his murdering dart,
> Who flies away at every glance I give,
> And, when I look away, comes stealing on.
> Villain, away, and hie thee to the field!
> I and mine army come to load thy back
> With souls of thousand mangled carcasses.
> Look, where he goes; but see, he comes again,
> Because I stay: Techelles, let us march
> And weary Death with bearing souls to hell.
>
> Part II, Act V, sc. iii.

But even in Marlowe the 'mighty line' is still felt as
the unit. All his volubility, his extravagance, his passion, his occasional tenderness did but develop the line
to its fullest possibilities; the larger unit of the long
harmonious period or ' blank verse paragraph ' is rare
and exceptional with him, though credit is due him for
foreshadowing this also:

> Now, lords, our loving friends and countrymen,
> Welcome to England all, with prosperous winds;
> Our kindest friends in Belgia have we left,
> To cope with friends at home; a heavy case
> When force to force is knit, and sword and glaive
> In civil broils make kin and countrymen
> Slaughter themselves in others, and their sides
> With their own weapons gored.
>
> Edward II, Act IV, sc. iv.

Shakespeare's blank verse is the supreme manifesta-
tion of the measure for dramatic purposes. In his plays
it modulates and adapts itself to the changing emotions

of every speaker, "from merely colloquial dialogue to strains of impassioned soliloquy, from comic repartee to tragic eloquence, from terse epigrams to elaborate descriptions." It is customary to distinguish three ' periods ' in Shakespeare's blank verse, corresponding closely to his whole artistic development: first, the more formal, ' single-moulded ' line of the early plays; second, the perfect freedom and mastery of the great tragedies; and, third, the daring liberties, verging on license, of the later plays. These distinctions have, of course, no more absolute value than all similar classifications of impalpable modifications, but they at least suggest the underlying truth that Shakespeare began as a beginner, and then, having mastered the difficulties and subtleties of the form, treated it with the easy familiarity of a master. To illustrate these developments adequately would require pages of quotation; but one may compare the restricted movement of such a passage as this from Two Gentlemen of Verona (III, i) —

> Proteus, I thank thee for thine honest care;
> Which to requite, command me while I live.
> This love of theirs myself have often seen,
> Haply when they have judg'd me fast asleep,
> And oftentimes have purpos'd to forbid
> Sir Valentine her company and my court;
> But, fearing lest my jealous aim might err,
> And so unworthily disgrace the man, —
> A rashness that I ever yet have shunn'd, —
> I gave him gentle looks, thereby to find
> That which thyself hast now disclos'd to me.

with the fine modulations, fitting exactly the nuances of meaning in this from Hamlet (III, iii) —

> May one be pardon'd and retain the offence?
> In the corrupted currents of this world
> Offence's gilded hand may shove by justice,
> And oft 'tis seen the wicked prize itself
> Buys out the law. But 'tis not so above.
> There is no shuffling, there the action lies
> In his true nature; and we ourselves compell'd,
> Even to the teeth and forehead of our faults,
> To give in evidence. What then? What rests?
> Try what repentance can. What can it not?

or this from King Lear (II, iv) —

> You see me here, you gods, a poor old man,
> As full of grief as age; wretched in both!
> If it be you that stirs these daughters' hearts
> Against their father, fool me not so much
> To bear it tamely; touch me with noble anger,
> And let not women's weapons, water-drops,
> Stain my man's cheeks.

and also with the flowing, slightly ' irregular ' lines of this from The Tempest (II, i) —

> But I feel not
> This deity in my bosom. Twenty consciences,
> That stand 'twixt me and Milan, candied be they
> And melt ere they molest! Here lies your brother,
> No better than the earth he lies upon
> If he were that which now he's like, that's dead;
> Whom I, with this obedient steel, three inches of it,
> Can lay to be for ever; whiles you, doing thus,
> To the perpetual wink for aye might put
> This ancient morsel, this Sir Prudence, who
> Should not upbraid our course.

The greater freedom of syncopation and substitution, of extra syllables and unusual pauses, which characterizes Shakespeare's later blank verse, became almost a norm with Beaumont and Fletcher, Shirley, Ford, and the Jacobean dramatists. They often carried freedom to the extreme limit, where an inch further would change verse into prose. They were capable, to be sure, of more careful regular verse, and wrote it when the occasion seemed to call for it; but partly from choice, and partly no doubt from haste or indifference or both, they made a very free blank verse their staple. Shakespeare had alternated prose and verse as the subject or tone required; the later dramatists seemed to seek a verse that might be, in a sense, midway between prose and verse. Thus they avoided a necessity of frequent change, except a loosening or tightening of the reins. To call this verse decadent is somewhat unjust. It is in truth a special form which is certainly well justified for certain subjects and occasions.

Why how darst thou meet me again thou rebel,
And knowst how thou hast used me thrice, thou rascal?
Were there not waies enough to fly my vengeance,
No hole nor vaults to hide thee from my fury,
But thou must meet me face to face to kill thee?
I would not seek thee to destroy thee willingly,
But now thou comest to invite me,
And comest upon me,
How like a sheep-biting rogue taken i'th' manner,
And ready for the halter dost thou look now!
Thou hast a hanging look thou scurvy thing, hast ne'er a knife
Nor ever a string to lead thee to Elysium?
   BEAUMONT and FLETCHER, Rule a Wife and Have a Wife, V, i.

By this you find I am to Millaine neer
Ally'd; but more to tempt your fury on
My life, know 'twas my valiant father took
Your brother prisoner, and presented him
Where he receiv'd his death, my father that
So oft hath humbled you in war, and made
His victories triumph almost upon
The ruines of your state.   DAVENANT, Love and Honour, V, iii.

When Milton composed Comus in 1634 it was natural for him to model his blank verse on the best of
Shakespeare's and Ben Jonson's, rather than on that of
the contemporary playwrights; for his finer taste, his
more delicate ear, and his classical training and tendencies would at once lead him to reject the metrical laxi-
ties of Ford, Shirley, Davenant, and the other writers of
' broken down ' blank verse. And though his language
shows great familiarity with the later plays of Shakespeare, especially The Tempest, he admitted comparatively few of their metrical licenses and followed in
the main the versification of the Midsummer Night's
Dream and the earlier tragedies. There is generally a
tendency to make the line the unit — but the verse
paragraph or stanza effect is also present in nearly
fully developed form, as witness the opening lines of
the poem — weak or feminine endings are not frequent, alexandrines very few. The ' short fit of rhyming ' (ll. 495 ff.), disapproved by Dr. Johnson, would
be explained partly by the tradition of the masque and
partly by the model of Shakespeare's comedies.

But the great Miltonic blank verse of Paradise Lost
is not a copy of any master; it is a development and a
consummation of two influences, the slow maturity of
Milton's mind, deepened and broadened by the Com-
monwealth controversies "not without dust and heat,"
and the exalted sublimity of the yet unattempted
theme of justifying God's management of human and
divine affairs. His maturity brought him his great
familiarity both in matter and in style with nearly all
that was best in European literature, and his peculiar

subject, with only gods and angels (Adam and Eve are scarcely human, even after the fall) for characters and selected portions of eternity and infinity for time and place, gave him the tendency to artificiality and strain to the outmost verges of sublimity, and to extraordinary involution of phrase and idea — for all of which he must have a suitable prosody. He chose blank verse when the poetical fashion was for rime and described it, in words not altogether clear, as consisting "only in apt numbers, fit quantity of syllables, and the sense variously drawn out from one verse to another." [1] Apt numbers, that is, appropriate rhythms, Milton's verse certainly has; but it is the last item, the great variety of movements subordinating the line-unit, and running-on of verses into longer periods, for which his blank verse is famous. Every page of Paradise Lost contains examples; some of the finest occur in the rhetorical display of the Pandemonic Council in Book II. Note the position of the pauses in the following passage, and then compare the specimens of early blank verse given above.

> Or could we break our way
> By force, and at our heels all hell should rise
> With blackest insurrection, to confound

[1] The main crux of this passage is "fit quantity of syllables." *Quantity* in such a context suggests syllabic length; and one recalls the sonnet to Lawes —

> not to scan
> With Midas' ears, committing short and long.

But, on the other hand, Mr. Robert Bridges has made it almost if not quite certain that Milton counted syllables, and therefore the phrase would mean "ten syllables to a line," proper allowance being made for elision. Since both interpretations agree pretty well with Milton's practice, one cannot be sure which he had in mind.

> Heaven's purest light, yet our great enemy
> All incorruptible would on his throne
> Sit unpolluted, and the ethereal mould
> Incapable of stain would soon expel
> Her mischief, and purge off the baser fire,
> Victorious.   II, 134–142.

On its formal side, what makes Milton's versification as unique as it is admirable, is the instinctive and yet prescient skill with which the pause is continuously varied so as to keep the whole metrical structure in movement. There are no dead lines. There are no jerks or stoppages. His movement may best be described by quoting a passage which, like many others, is at once a description and an instance. It is a

> Mystical dance, which yonder starry sphere
> Of planets and of fixt in all her wheels
> Resembles nearest, mazes intricate,
> Eccentric, intervolv'd, yet regular
> Then most, when most irregular they seem,
> And in their motions harmony divine.

I ask the reader most particularly to notice that these six lines, like almost any short quotation that can be made from the poem, are broken from their context. They begin in the middle of a sentence, and end in the middle of a clause. The continuous periodic movement cannot be really shown by examples, just because it is continuous and periodic. If we except the speeches, each of which by the necessity of the case is more or less a definite and detachable unit, the periods flow into one another. Like the orbit of a planet, the movement of the verse never closes its ellipse and begins again. Each of the twelve books is a single organic rhythmical structure. But one cannot very well quote a whole book.

Within that structure, the variation of pause and stress is similarly in continuous movement. As a general fact, this is instinctively felt in reading the poem; how rigorously the law of freedom is observed comes out even more surprisingly when brought to the test of figures. For movement of stress one instance may serve as a typical example. In Michael's description of the plagues of Egypt in the twelfth book, beginning —

> But first the lawless tyrant, who denies
> To know their God, or message to regard,
> Must be compelled by signs and judgments dire —

the detailed roll of the plagues is all threaded on the word *must*. It recurs nine times, with studied and intricate variation of its place in the line: this is, taken by order, in the first, eighth, fifth, fourth, fifth, fifth, first, third, and fourth syllable. Again, as regards variation, in the whole ten thousand lines of the Paradise Lost there are less than five-and-twenty instances of the pause coming at the same point in the line for more than two lines consecutively. Facts like these are the formal index of what is the great organic principle of Milton's verse. That is, that like all organic structures, it is incalculable; it cannot be reduced to a formula. . . . His rhythm is perpetually integrating as it advances; and not only so, but at no point can its next movement be predicted, although tracing it backwards we can see how each phrase rises out of and carries on the rhythm of what was before it, how each comes in not only rightly, but as it seems inevitably. This secret he inherited from no English predecessor and transmitted to no follower.[1]

One may surely say that Milton extracted from blank verse all its possibilities of variety and movement so far as his subject matter permitted. He is lyrical, dramatic, didactic, and of course epic, in turn. He even showed that it is possible to imitate hollowly his own "planetary wheelings" — as though the instruments kept on playing and the music ceased.[2]

Since Paradise Regained and Samson Agonistes, though various poets have adapted it to their own uses, blank verse has shown only one significant development, the conversational, or so-called ' talking,' style. In the eighteenth century Milton's mannerisms

[1] J. W. Mackail, The Springs of Helicon, pp. 181 ff.
[2] Cf., for example, Paradise Regained, III, 68 ff.

dominated nearly all blank verse, both for good and for evil. What freedom Thomson allowed himself he got from Milton; most of Cowper's thin grandiosity he took from Milton; and much also of Wordsworth's false and empty elaboration which make the Prelude and Excursion so dull in places — the whole tribe of verses of which

> And at the Hoop alighted, famous inn

is the pilloried example — came from the Miltonic tradition. Keats fell partially into the error, but was wise enough to recognize it. Shelley, with much of Milton's intensity and somewhat too of his sublimity, could successfully follow the great stride and at the same time preserve his own idiom. Tennyson, keeping both the freedom and as much of the "continuous planetary movement" as was consistent with his themes, softened the metre — weakened it, some will say — by his decorative tendency and indulgence in only half-concealed virtuosity.[1] And the famous Oxus ending of Arnold's Sohrab and Rustum is a studied reproduction of the Miltonic music in a lower key. But it was Landor who, taking a hint perhaps from Milton's unadorned didacticism of Paradise Regained and also from the straightforward verse used on occasion by the Elizabethan dramatists, showed the way to what has often been called a strictly contemporary development of blank verse, the talking style. Since this is less

---

[1] Browning's blank verse, like all his metres, is typically Browningesque; instead of moulding his verse to fit the idea perfectly, he too often effected the compromise between content and form by slighting the latter.

familiar than most of the phenomena of blank verse, it will require fuller illustration.

The uneven line which separates blank verse and prose is easily apparent in such a passage as the following from Much Ado about Nothing (V, i) —

Leon.	Some haste, my lord! — well, fare you well, my lord: —
	Are you so hasty now — Well, all is one.
D. Pedro.	Nay, do not quarrel with us, good old man.
Ant.	If he could right himself with quarrelling,
	Some of us would lie low.
Claud.	Who wrongs him?
Leon.	Marry, thou dost wrong me; thou dissembler, thou. —
	Nay, never lay thy hand upon thy sword;
	I fear thee not.
Claud.	Marry, beshrew my hand,
	If it should give your age such cause of fear.
	In faith, my hand meant nothing to my sword.
Leon.	Tush, tush, man! never fleer and jest at me;
	I speak not like a dotard nor a fool;
	As under privilege of age, to brag
	What I have done being young, or what would do,
	Were I not old. Know, Claudio, to thy heed,
	Thou hast so wrong'd mine innocent child and me,
	That I am forc'd to lay my reverence by,
	And with gray hairs and bruise of many days,
	Do challenge thee to trial of a man. . . .

In the first part of this passage the language is the simple natural expression of prose, yet so devised that it also fits the metrical pattern. It is either prose or verse according to the way one reads it. But in Leonardo's long speech (after the first line, which is ' irregular ') the verse pattern becomes more and more prominent, until in the last three lines it predominates over the natural utterance of the words and produces a certain stiffness. Here the two different manners stand side by side: a natural simplicity so great that the metrical quality is almost obscured, beside a formality so obvious that the feeling of natural expression is partly lost. Now Milton, and after him Dryden and the eighteenth century, regarding poetry generally as a thing apart, followed the latter sort; but when the Romantic Revival brought poetry back to ordinary human life there reappeared, tentatively, of course, a simpler blank verse in Thomson, Crabbe, Cowper, and Wordsworth. A clear example is the opening of Landor's Iphigeneia and Agamemnon —

> Iphigeneia, when she heard her doom
> At Aulis, and when all beside the King
> Had gone away, took his right hand, and said,
> "O father! I am young and very happy.
> I do not think the pious Calchas heard
> Distinctly what the Goddess spake. Old-age
> Obscures the senses. If my nurse, who knew
> My voice so well, sometimes misunderstood
> While I was resting on her knee both arms
> And hitting it to make her mind my words,
> And looking in her face, and she in mine,
> Might he not also hear one word amiss,
> Spoken from so far off, even from Olympus?"

Again, compare Mrs. Browning's Aurora Leigh —

> As it was, indeed,
> I felt a mother-want about the world,
> And still went seeking, like a bleating lamb
> Left out at night, in shutting up the fold, —
> As restless as a nest-deserted bird
> Grown chill through something being away, though what
> It knows not. I, Aurora Leigh, was born
> To make my father sadder, and myself
> Not overjoyous, truly. Women know
> The way to rear up children (to be just),

They know a simple, merry, tender knack
Of tying sashes, fitting baby-shoes,
And stringing pretty words that make no sense,
And kissing full sense into empty words.

These are from the metrical point of view nearly identical with Mr. Robert Frost's talking verse, so often called a 'contribution' to verse technique —

Something there is that doesn't love a wall,
That sends the frozen ground-swell under it,
And spills the upper boulders in the sun;
And makes gaps even two can pass abreast.
The work of hunters is another thing:
I have come after them and made repair
Where they have left not one stone on stone,
But they would have the rabbit out of hiding,
To please the yelping dogs.   R. FROST, Mending Wall.[1]

The obvious difficulty is to maintain dignity along with relaxation — a feat which Mr. Frost and Mr. E. A. Robinson have occasionally accomplished. And from this it is but a step to the extreme simplicity of Miss Lowell's To Two Unknown Ladies —

If either of you much attracted me
We could fall back upon phenomena
And make a pretty story out of psychic
Balances, but not to be too broad
In my discourtesy, nor prudish neither
(Since, really, I can hardly quite suppose
With all your ghostliness you follow me),
I feel no such attraction. Or if one
Bows to my sympathy for the briefest space,

[1] Mr. Frost in some of his later work permits himself such laxness as —

Had beauties he had to point out to me at length
To insure their not being wasted on me.
                                        The Axe-Helve.

> Snap — it is gone! And, worst of all to tell,
> What broke it is not in the least dislike
> But utter boredom.
> Now. . . .

Thus the wheel has come nearly full circle, but with a longer radius. For just as blank verse developed from the early Elizabethan — and pre-Elizabethan — strict formality to the laxity of the Jacobean dramatists and found a true balance of freedom and restraint in Milton, so from the monotonous eighteenth-century couplet (and it should be recalled that in the beginning blank verse sprang from the couplet) it has gradually enlarged its freedom into the extreme license from a metrical point of view of its adopted cousin free-verse. Already, moreover, there have been signs of a reaction against the extreme, and the wheel is coming to an artistic balance again.

4. FREE-VERSE

Free-verse (or, as Miss Lowell prefers, ' unrhymed cadence ') is a hydra-headed phenomenon. It can never be adequately discussed; for when one head is disposed of, two others appear in its place. Its origins are involved in obscurity and — what is worse — ignorance; and its practitioners and staunchest defenders are as variable in their points of view as it itself is in its rhythmic impulses.[1]

---

[1] Strongly to be deprecated is the frequent confusion not only of the different varieties of English free-verse, but of the fundamentally distinct phenomena of free-verse as commonly understood and French *vers libre*. *Vers libre* itself has many aspects, from the literally freer use of rime and the mute *-e* than the traditional French prosody allowed and an escape from the old principle of syllabification to what superficially corresponds

Behind all the utterances of friend and foe seems to lie the ultimate belief that the ' voluntary thraldom ' of formal metrical patterns is a monstrous error which can only be removed by unrestricted appreciation and application of the natural rhythms of idea and of language. There is in every thought, however simple or subtle, in every feeling, however evanescent or profound, an inherent rhythm which is as a material body to the thought's or emotion's soul. This native, inevitable rhythm — one might call it the *rhythme juste*, the exact rhythm—is the only fit expression for an intellectual or emotional idea; all others are foreign to it, tyrannous usurpations, in a word, impossible substitutions for it. To attempt, therefore, to twist these natural and exact rhythms to the formal predetermined patterns of traditional versification is a suicidal impertinence, foredoomed to failure.

Such a position has in theory much justice. It means briefly that the basis of poetical form should not be the metrical pattern freely varied yet always perceptible, but the natural organic rhythm of the ideas expressed; that is, there should be no harmonized difference between what have been explained above as thought rhythms, sound rhythms, and metrical rhythms, but all three should be one original and indivisible unit. This would make a combined thought-and-sound unit (breath group and logical-emotional

---

with English free-verse, that is, a substitution of prose for verse; but only superficially, since the French language is phonetically different from English, and its ordinary prose has a naturally greater song potentiality. Since the phenomena differ they should not be called by the same name. The English term ' free-verse ' is wholly adequate.

group) the foundation of verse, whereas this is really the characteristic of prose as distinguished from verse. These exact organic rhythms "differ from ordinary prose rhythms," says Miss Lowell, "in being more curved, and containing more stress"; which, though not very perspicuous, seems to mean that free-verse is more carefully cadenced, or, in other words, more nearly metrical, than ordinary prose. Perhaps it would be no injustice to the upholders of free-verse in its best manifestations to say that, while metre requires that beneath all variations the regular beat should never be missed, free-verse requires as much rhythm (i. e., regularity) as is possible without its becoming perceptible.

If this is true, or as near the manifold truth as one can get, then the free-verse movement in English is mainly a return to the cadenced prose of the seventeenth century with the additional trait of the appearance of verse. This is an important addition, however. It involves a careful recognition of what psychology calls the ' prose attitude ' and the ' verse attitude,' and also (as has been suggested above) the peculiar union of prose with the spatial rhythm of verse. We read with ear and eye together, though with varying proportions of emphasis on the one or the other; for some ' vocalize ' whatever they read, others read almost entirely with the eye. Since it is the eye that takes the earlier and quicker perception of printed language, we tend to judge by the appearance of a page whether it contains prose or verse. Columns of irregular but approximately equal line lengths, regular blocks of printing regularly spaced and separated as stanzas, indentation of every second or every third line — these at once announce that the page contains verse. And they at the same time constitute an obvious spatial rhythm to the eye, and prepare the attention of eye and ear and mind for the approximate regularity of verse. Then, when so prepared, we unconsciously organize as fully as possible any irregularities that appear in the language and transform into actual verse the verse potentialities which pervade our speech.

Some kinds of free-verse, however, do not, so far as one can see, aim to be more than ordinary prose printed in segments more or less closely corresponding with the phrase rhythm or normal sound rhythms of language. It is then prose in actuality and verse in appearance — no more.

On the justification of this peculiar amalgam there is little agreement. No doubt for certain swift effects free-verse is the natural and most serviceable medium. Many short poems in this irregular form are like snap-shots or like rapid sketches as compared with finished paintings. But the ultimate æsthetic judgment must be precisely that of the snapshot as compared with finished painting. Nature is always wrong, says the paradox; art depends upon a deliberate selection of details and structure. It balances freedom and restraint, variety and uniformity, one against the other; and even when it appears spontaneous it is but the result of an unconscious choice which is itself born of long training or of the mysterious faculty divine. In very little of what at present is called free-verse does art have a real place. It is all freedom and variety, with almost no restraint and uniformity: all stimulation and no repose. There is sometimes a rapid alternation of verse rhythm and prose rhythm, which, in Bacon's phrase, may cleave but not incorporate; they succeed each other but do not melt into each other. Now and again, to be sure, this uncertainty, this very irregularity, powerfully represents the thought and emotion of the poem; but nevertheless there can be little doubt that except in the limited field of instantaneous flashes the most adequate and pleasing medium is the skilfully varied regularity of formal verse.[1]

The many kinds of free-verse are recognizable chiefly by the greater or less feeling of metrical form lying behind them. For convenience they may be distinguished, according as verse or prose predominates, as (1) irregular unrimed metre, (2) very free blank verse, (3) unusual mingling of metre and prose, a kind of recitative, and (4) mere prose printed as verse, or what may be called free-verse *par excellence*. A few illustrations will help to make clear the distinctions.

Of the first sort are the unrimed choruses in Milton's Samson Agonistes, the metre of Southey's once-

---

[1] "In the effort to get rhyme, ' the rack of finest wits,' " says a pseudonymous newspaper writer, "and in the struggle, writhing, and agony of trying to get the wrong words to say the right thing, one sometimes achieves the impossible, or, rather, from the flame of frantic friction (of ' Rhyming Dictionary ' leaves) rises, phoenix-like, another idea, somewhat like the first, its illegitimate child, so to say, and thus more beautiful.

"With vers libre one experiences the mortification one sometimes feels in having roared out one's agony in perfectly fit terms. With rhymed poetry one feels the satisfaction of a wit who gives the nuance of his meaning by the raise of an eyebrow, the turn of a word."

admired Thalaba and the Curse of Kehama, and parts
of Shelley's Queen Mab. Here the lines are irregular in
length (as in the ' irregular ' Pindaric odes), but they
are usually felt as truly metrical, though they do not
repeat a single pattern.

> This, this is he; softly a while;
> Let us not break in upon him.
> O change beyond report, thought, or belief!
> See how he lies at random, carelessly diffused,
> With languished head unpropt,
> As one past hope, abandoned,
> And by himself given over,
> In slavish habit, ill-fitted weeds
> O'er-worn and soiled.
> Or do mine eyes misrepresent?   Can this be he,
> That heroic, that renowned,
> Irresistible Samson? . . .
>
> > Samson Agonistes, 115–126.

> The Fairy waved her wand:
> Ahasuerus fled
> Fast as the shapes of mingled shade and mist
> That lurk in the glens of a twilight grove
> Flee from the morning beam:
> The matter of which dreams are made
> Not more endowed with actual life
> Than this phantasmal portraiture
> Of wandering human thought.
>
> > Queen Mab, iii.

> Thou tyrannous over-mastering Spirit, Lucifer,
> Hear now thy guilt.
> The first in glory amongst us all wast thou;
> Nor did we grudge thee loyalty,
> When of old beneath thy leadership against Yahveh,
> And thereafter against the mild Galilean Godhead,
> We waged war for dominion over the minds of man.
> But perished now long since is the might of Yahveh;
> And his Son, a plaintive, impotent phantom, wails

> Over that faith, withering, corrupted, petrified,
> For which he died vainly.
>
>   R. C. Trevelyan, Lucifer Enchained.

> Green boughs stirring in slumber
> Sigh at the lost remembrance
> Of Aulon,
> Golden-thighed, in the heart of the forest.

> Here, where the dripping leaves
> Whisper of passing feet
> To the fragrant woodways,
> The moonlight floods the forsaken tangled boughs
> With loneliness
> For Melinna, gone from the evening.
>
>   Edward J. O'Brien, Hellenica.

Very free blank verse, when taken in small excerpts, often seems devoid of metrical regularity. The reason for this is that in long poems much greater freedom is possible because the ear and the attention, accustomed for longer periods to the formal pattern, hold it more easily where it becomes faint. Examples of this approximation to prose have been given above, pages 43, 44. The famous first lines of Paradise Lost, if printed after the contemporary fashion of free-verse, would by very few be recognized as blank verse; and the same is true of many passages throughout the poem, and indeed throughout all long poems in blank verse.

> Of Man's first disobedience
> And the fruit of that forbidden tree
> Whose mortal taste brought death into the world,
> And all our woe,
> With loss of Eden,
> Till one greater Man restore us
> And regain the blissful seat,
> Sing,

Heavenly Muse,
That on the secret top of Horeb
Or of Sinai
Didst inspire that shepherd . . .

Among the finest free-verse in English are the Evening Voluntaries of Henley.[1] In these poems clearly metrical lines (sometimes only parts of lines) alternate with simple prose. The line length is now based on phrasal rhythm, and at other times on no discoverable principle except that of beginning a new line with some emphatic word.

White fleets of cloud,
Argosies heavy with fruitfulness,
Sail the blue peacefully.　Green flame the hedgerows.
Blackbirds are bugling, and white in wet winds
Sway the tall poplars.
Pageants of colour and fragrance,
Pass the sweet meadows, and viewless
Walks the mild spirit of May,
Visibly blessing the world.　　　HENLEY, Pastoral.

Have the gods then left us in our need
Like base and common men?
Were even the sweet grey eyes
Of Artemis a lie,
The speech of Hermes but a trick,
The glory of Apollonian hair deceit?

Desolate we move across a desolate land,
The high gates closed,
No answer to our prayer;
Naught left save our integrity,
No murmur against Fate
Save that we are juster than the unjust gods,
More pitiful than they.
　　　RICHARD ALDINGTON, Disdain.

[1] See a part of Margaritæ Sorori, page 43, above.

Modern free-verse, or free-verse *par excellence*, which is mere prose with the spatial rhythm of verse, has been skilfully written by various contemporaries. Let a single example suffice. Such a bare but moving situation as that of Miss Lowell's Fool's Money Bags could no doubt be adequately presented in traditional metre, but perhaps not so directly as in her ' curved ' prose —

> Outside the long window,
> With his head on the stone sill,
> The dog is lying,
> Gazing at his Beloved.
> His eyes are wet and urgent,
> And his body is taut and shaking.
> It is cold on the terrace;
> A pale wind licks along the stone slabs,
> But the dog gazes through the glass
> And is content.
>
> The Beloved is writing a letter.
> Occasionally she speaks to the dog,
> But she is thinking of her writing.
> Does she, too, give her devotion to one
> Not worthy?[1]

A good example of combined metre and confessed prose (not to be confused with the mingling of verse and prose illustrated on the previous page) with easy transitions from one form to the other may be seen in a poem called Spring by Mr. Clement Wood. The rapid change from verse to prose is, of course, familiar in Shakespeare and his fellow dramatists, sometimes even in a single speech.

---

[1] From Sword Blades and Poppy Seeds, by permission of Houghton Mifflin Co.

5. Exotic Forms

As wide as are the possibilities of variety in native English verse, the poets have endeavored to extend its boundaries by the annexation of foreign prosodies from ancient Greece and Rome and from mediaeval France. In absolute contrast to free-verse, which is the denial of metrical formalism, this is the apotheosis of it. They admittedly place form above content and are satisfied (for the most part) with the mere exhilaration of dancing gracefully in chains.

A group of Elizabethan experimenters, among whom were Sidney and Spenser, sought diligently to compose in the quantitative metres of the classics; Puttenham, the author of one of the first English treatises on the Art of Poetry (1589), declared that by "leisurable travail" one might "easily and commodiously lead all those feet of the ancients into our vulgar language"; but while they may have satisfied themselves (Spenser certainly did not) these experimenters produced nothing of genuine significance. The result was candidly anticipated by Ascham, who said in the Schoolmaster (1570) that "*carmen exametrum* doth rather trot and hobble than run smoothly in our English tongue." Thomas Nash confirms this opinion in his criticism of Stanyhurst's attempt to translate Virgil into hexameters: "The hexameter verse I grant to be a gentleman of an ancient house (so is many an English beggar); yet this clime of ours he cannot thrive in. Our speech is too craggy for him to set his plow in. He goes twitching and hopping in our language like a man running upon quagmires, up the hill in one syllable and

down the dale in another, retaining no part of that
stately smooth gait which he vaunts himself with
amongst the Greeks and Latins " (Four Letters Con-
futed). Coleridge's judgment was the same:

This is a galloping measure, a hop, and a trot, and a gallop.

Thereafter, apart from isolated attempts, efforts
were abandoned until the nineteenth century, when
Southey, following William Taylor, who in turn had
been induced by Goethe's Hermann und Dorothea to
try a new principle of frankly substituting sentence
stress or accent for length of syllable, wrote his Vision
of Judgment (1821). Out of this revised experimenting
came ultimately Longfellow's Evangeline (1847) and
the Courtship of Miles Standish (1858) and Clough's
Bothie of Tober-na-Vuolich (1848). These alone, not
to mention the lesser imitations, were enough to dis-
credit the movement metrically. Meanwhile Tennyson and Kingsley, followed later by William Watson,
and still enthusiastically by the present Poet Laureate,
undertook to harmonize syllabic length and stress by
more or less occult processes. As a matter of learned
experiment and debate these problems have a certain
academic interest, but only the staunchest and (one
may say) blindest adherents find in them any practical
importance.

The storm centre of all classical adaptations has
been the dactylic hexameter, the standard measure of
Greek and Latin narrative poetry. The most nearly
successful English hexameters are probably those of
Kingsley's Andromeda (1858), which occupy a middle

ground between the purely accentual and the purely (so-called) quantitative experiments. An example of this and one of Mr. Bridges' quantitative hexameters must suffice. Though both have good qualities, neither approaches the melodic variety and dignity of Homer and Virgil, or even Ovid.[1]

Over the sea, past Crete, on the Syrian shore to the southward,
Dwells in the well-tilled lowland a dark-haired Æthiop people,
Skilful with needle and loom, and the arts of the dyer and carver,
Skilful, but feeble of heart; for they know not the lords of
    Olympus,
Lovers of men; neither broad-browed Zeus, nor Pallas Athené,
Teacher of wisdom to heroes, bestower of might in the battle;
Share not the cunning of Hermes, nor list to the songs of Apollo.
                                                    Andromeda.

Now in wintry delights, and long fireside meditation,
'Twixt studies and routine paying due court to the Muses,
My solace in solitude, when broken roads barricade me
Mudbound, unvisited for months with my merry children,
Grateful t'ward Providence, and heeding a slander against me
Less than a rheum, think of me to-day, dear Lionel, and take
This letter as some account of Will Stone's versification.
                            R. BRIDGES, Wintry Delights.

After the hexameter the most frequently imitated metre is the Sapphic strophe. Swinburne's Sapphics in Poems and Ballads are the best known; but though they are finely musical they do not pretend to give more than an echo of the Greek music.

All the night sleep came not upon my eyelids,
Shed not dew, nor shook nor unclosed a feather,

[1] The advanced student should of course read carefully the paper on " Classical Metres in English " by W. J. Stone in Bridges' Milton's Prosody (2d ed.), pp. 113 ff.   Mr. Stone regards the hexameters of Clough's Actæon and some specimen verses by Spedding (the biographer of Bacon) as the best he has seen.

Yet with lips shut close and with eyes of iron
  Stood and beheld me.

Then to me so lying awake a vision
Came without sleep over the seas and touched me,
Softly touched mine eyelids and lips; and I too,
  Full of the vision,

Saw the white implacable Aphrodite,
Saw the hair unbound and the feet unsandalled
Shine as fire of sunset on western waters;
  Saw the reluctant. . . .

Both Tennyson and Swinburne tried the Catullan
hendecasyllabics. Tennyson's Milton, in alcaics, is
famous, and has a well-marked Miltonic sound, but
little of the sound of Horace's alcaics. Admirable also
are the elegiac distichs of Watson's Hymn to the
Sea —

Man whose deeds, to the doer, come back as thine own exhala-
  tions
  Into thy bosom return, weepings of mountain and vale;
Man with the cosmic fortunes and starry vicissitudes tangled,
  Chained to the wheel of the world, blind with the dust of its
  speed,
Even as thou, O giant, whom trailed in the wake of her conquests
  Night's sweet despot draws, bound to her ivory car.

Of the French lyrical metres that have been imitated
in English, mainly for lighter themes, the *ballade* and
the *rondeau* are the most important. These and the
villanelle, *triolet*, and *pantoum* are not, like imitations of
classical forms, semi-learned attempts to do in English
what is foreign to the nature of the language, but games
of skill in phrasing and riming, wholly legitimate once
their artificiality is granted. For the impassioned overflowing of a sincere spirit they are unfitted, but for

grace, point, and delicate charm nothing could be better devised; and when occasionally they are used for the expression of genuine feeling, the unexpected union of lightness and seriousness has a peculiarly poignant effect.

The *ballade* in its commonest form consists of three 8-line stanzas riming *ababbcbc* and a 4-line stanza called 'envoy,' *bcbc*; the last line of each stanza being repeated as a refrain, and the *a*, *b*, and *c* rimes throughout the poem being the same. The lines contain usually either four or five stresses. The envoy is a sort of dedication, addressed traditionally to a "Prince." Variations of all kinds occur, encouraged by the difficulty of satisfying all the demands of the form. Examples may be found (with an excellent introduction) in Gleeson White's collection of Ballades and Rondeaus (Canterbury Poets), and Andrew Lang's Ballades of Blue China.

Rondeaus and *rondels* (two forms of the same word) are written with greater freedom of variation. Their organic principle is the use of the first phrase or first line, twice repeated, as a refrain (R). The commoner model in English is: *aabba, aabR, aabbaR*, in which the first half of the first line constitutes the refrain. Another type rimes *ABba, abAB, abbaAB* (the capital letters indicating the lines repeated). For examples see the reference above. Austin Dobson, Henley, and Swinburne have written successfully in this form.

The *triolet* is a sort of abbreviation of the second variety of rondeau. Its lines are usually short and rime *ABaAabAB*.

The *villanelle*, in its normal form, consists of five 3-line stanzas (*aba*) and a concluding 4-line stanza, all with but two rimes, the first line, moreover, being repeated as the sixth, twelfth, and eighteenth, the third line as the ninth, fifteenth, and nineteenth.

The *pantoum* is of Eastern origin, but it came into English through the French. It is extremely rare. It consists of a series of quatrains *abab*, with the second and fourth lines of each stanza repeated chainwise as the first and third of the next stanza. The closing stanza completes the chain by taking as its second and fourth lines the first and third of the first stanza.

From Italy have come, besides the *ottava rima* and the sonnet, two other metrical forms, the *sestina* and the *terza rima*. The sestina is composed of six 6-line stanzas and a final 3-line stanza. Instead of rimes the end words of the lines of the first stanza are repeated in this order 1.2.3.4.5.6. — 6.1.5.2.4.3. — 3.6.4.1.2.5. — 5.3.2.6.1.4. — 4.5.1.3.6.2. — 2.4.6.5.3.1. — and the last stanza 5.3.1. with 2.4.6. in the middle of the lines. Gosse, Swinburne, and Kipling have written sestinas; Swinburne one with the additional embellishment of rime.

The *terza rima* is the metre of Dante's Divine Comedy. The rimes are *aba*, *bcb*, *cdc*, etc. . . . *yzy*, *zz*. It has not been very successfully used in English, except in the stanzaic arrangement of Shelley's Ode to the West Wind, — *aba*, *bcb*, *cdc*, *ded*, *ee*. Other examples besides translations of Dante are short poems by Wyatt and Sidney, Browning's The Statue and the Bust, and Shelley's unfinished The Triumph of Life.

CHAPTER V

MELODY, HARMONY, AND MODULATION

THE terms melody, harmony, and modulation, being borrowed from music, are not to be applied too literally to the art of versification. They represent metaphorically, however, certain important qualities of verse which, with the exception of rime, cannot from their very impalpability be formally explained, but can only be suggested and partially described. They are not the determining and fundamental characteristics of verse — those have already been discussed — but rather its sources of incremental beauty, of richness and subtle power. To draw an illustration from another art, they add light and shadow, fullness, roundness, depth of perspective, vividness, to what would else be simple line-drawing.

The language of ordinary prose has its own melody and harmony, its own sonorous rhythms, and its own delicate adjustments between sound and meaning. All these natural beauties verse inherits from prose and then adds the further beauties that result from the union of prose rhythms and the formal patterns of verse. Some of these qualities which are the peculiar enhancements of verse will now be examined.

The simplest and most tangible of these is rime in its various forms. Rime is, in its most general signification, the repetition, usually at regulated intervals,

of identical or closely similar sounds. According to
the circumstances of the identical or similar sounds,
four varieties are distinguishable: (1) *alliteration*, or
initial rime, when the sounds at the beginning of accented syllables agree, as *t*ale, a*t*tune; (2) *consonance*,
when the vowel sounds differ and the final consonantal
sounds agree, as ta*l*e, pu*ll*; (3) *assonance*, when the
vowel sounds agree and the consonants differ, as t*a*le,
p*ai*n; and (4) *rime proper*, when both the vowels and
the final consonants agree, as t*ale*, p*ale*.

Alliteration is a natural and obvious method of
emphasis in English — and often difficult to avoid
rather than to obtain. Popular sayings — wind and
weather, time and tide, kith and kin, ever and aye, to
have and to hold — are fond of it for its own sake. The
early English, German, and Scandinavian prosodies
made it a determining principle; and in the north of
England it survived well into the fifteenth century;
but since then it has been considered a too 'easy' kind
of metrical ornament, one to be used sparingly and
only for very special effects. "Apt alliteration's artful
aid" is very well when it is apt and artful; but when
some poets in their simplicity have gone so far as to
"hunt the letter to the death," one cannot but con-
demn it, in John Burroughs' ironic phrase, as a "lep-
rosy of alliteration." Most of the poets, however, have
made skilful use of it, notably Tennyson and Swinburne, though the latter frequently overdid it, as in —

. . . rusted sheaves
Rain-rotten in rank lands.

A Ballad of Death.

Very remarkable is the combination of rime and frequent alliteration in Browning's Abt Vogler.

Analogous to alliteration and perhaps to be classed as a by-form of it is the subtle use of the same sound in unstressed parts of neighboring words, as in —

> Over the dark abyss, whose boi*l*ing gu*l*f
> Tame*l*y endured a bridge of wondrous *l*ength.
>
> Paradise Lost, II, 1027–28.

Consonance is very similar to this latter form of alliteration. Its use is irregular and usually hidden. Note the alliteration and consonance in Milton's line, both the *s*'s and the *n*'s —

> Through the soft silence of the list'ning night.

Assonance, like alliteration and consonance, occurs in modern verse sporadically, almost accidentally, but with great frequency in all languages. As a regular principle of verse (in place of rime) it is characteristic of Spanish and of Old French; in English its deliberate use is very rare—the best example is perhaps the song "Bright, O bright Fedalma" in George Eliot's The Spanish Gypsy.

Minute analysis is tedious and unsatisfactory, often indeed misleading, but a single example will perhaps suggest some of the ways in which alliteration, consonance, and assonance are interwoven for harmonic effects that, not being altogether obvious, are felt rather than directly perceived. Similar experiments may be made by the reader with other passages. The opening stanza of Gray's Elegy, quoted on page 55, above, is remarkable for its smooth and quiet flow, symbolic of the atmosphere described by the words. How is this ' atmosphere ' produced? or rather, what is there that produces in us this sense of appropriate atmosphere? In the first place, the lines are 5-stress and have the "long iambic roll," and the rimes are simple *abab*. Furthermore, the coincidence of prose and verse rhythms is noticeable; there are only three variations: *wind* in the second line, which is too important to occupy the metrically unstressed position, and *o'er* in the second line and the second *and* in the fourth, which are not quite strong enough to stand in the stressed position. By a sort of substitution or ' occult balance ' the weakness of *o'er* is compensated by the slight overweight of *wind*. And the weakness of *and* is strengthened by the rhetorical pause after *darkness*. A rough approximation in semi-musical notation would give for the second line

$$\smile \; \bar{} \; \smile \; \bar{} \; \bar{} \; \bar{} \; \smile \; \smile \; \smile \; \bar{}$$

There is a syncopation by which $-\,-$ and $\smile \; \smile$ combine (the natural syllabic length of *o'er* helping considerably) without destroying the fundamental rhythm. In the fourth line, instead of

$$\smile \; \bar{} \; \smile \; \bar{} \; \smile \; \bar{}$$

we have

$$\smile \quad \bar{} \quad \smile \; \wedge \; \smile \; \smile \; \bar{}$$
$$\ldots \text{ to dark-ness and to me,} \, \text{—}$$

the pause being supported by the meaning as well as by the structure of the verse. Alliteration is appropriately inconspicuous; it is limited to *pl*owman . . . *pl*ods and the conventional *w*eary *w*ay. The consonance is

significant. The most frequently repeated consonantal
sounds are: *l* 10, *d* 9, *r*[1] 8, *th* 6, *n* 6, and *w* 5; that is, of
the seventy consonantal sounds (counting *th* as one, *p*
and *l* as two sounds) in the stanza, thirty-five, or one-
half, are the comparatively soft sounds *l*, *r*, *th*, *n*, *w*.
From the point of view of the line, a tabulation shows
two or more occurrences in each line of —

```
1 — TH R T L
2 — TH·R   L D
3 —    R   L D P M W H
4 —    R T L D           N
```

That is, there is a kind of RTLD motif throughout the
stanza. The assonance is even more striking. The
stressed vowel sounds (which are of course the most
important [2]) line by line are as follows: [3]

```
ŭ ͬ ō ĕ ā ē
ō ŭ ͬ ō ō ī
au ō ŏ ī ē
ī ŭ ͬ ā ī
```

Here the five ō-sounds and four ī-sounds and three
ŭ ͬ-sounds are noticeable.

Now while no one would dream of saying that such a
mechanical examination unlocks the mystery of this
quatrain's music, it cannot be denied that the predominance of some sounds (especially those that are
peculiarly suggestive) over others is significant. And
certainly such a tabulation reveals *parts* of the mystery
which are not plain even to the trained eye and ear.

---

[1] According to the commonest American pronunciation.
[2] The unaccented vowel sounds show the usual predominance of the
obscure vowel e, with three occurrences of I and ĭ.
[3] Reference to the text will identify the symbols.

The origin of rime is much disputed, but it occurs, at least sporadically, in the poetry of nearly all peoples, and is likely to have been a spontaneous growth arising from a natural human pleasure in similar sounds. "It lies deep in our human nature and satisfies an universal need." It is an established phenomenon in Sanskrit and Persian prosody, in Arabic, in Chinese, in Celtic, in Icelandic. Greek prosody, and Latin, which was based upon Greek, rejected it, partly perhaps because it was too simple an ornament for the highly cultivated Greek taste, especially on account of the great frequency of similar inflectional endings, and perhaps because it was not entirely consistent with the quantitative principle.[1] In the *popular* Latin verse, however, which was accentual, rime is found; and when, before the fall of the later Empire, quantity was gradually abandoned, rime returned as a regular feature of Latin verse. From thence it passed into the Romance languages — Provençal, Italian, French — where it was for a time rivalled by assonance; and finally, under French influence after the Conquest, it made its way into England. But it had not been unknown in earliest English verse, though it occurred only here and there, as in Greek and Latin.[2] And from the fact that rimes appear with greater frequency in the later than in the earlier Anglo-Saxon verse, as the native poets became more

---

[1] Rime occurs, however, here and there in Greek and Latin poetry, and is more frequent than perhaps we commonly suppose.

[2] In the 3182 lines of Beowulf, for example, there are sixteen exact rimes and many more approximate rimes. There is also in Anglo-Saxon the so-called Riming Poem, of uncertain date, composed probably under Scandinavian influence.

familiar with the rimed Latin hymns, one may feel sure that it would have developed into a staple of English verse independently of French influence. From the twelfth century until the introduction of blank verse by the Elizabethans, practically all English verse, except that which belongs to the Alliterative Revival (mainly in the north of England) of the second half of the fourteenth century, was rimed.

From the æsthetic point of view rime has been severely attacked and faithfully defended. A lively controversy was waged at the end of the sixteenth century between the Renaissance classicists, who of course condemned it, and the native rimers, but was brought to a peaceful conclusion by Samuel Daniels' A Defence of Rhyme in 1603. In a prefatory note to the second edition of Paradise Lost, Milton delivered an arrogant but ineffectual counterblast. Rime, he said, was "no necessary adjunct or true ornament of poem or good verse, in longer works especially, but the invention of a barbarous age, to set off wretched matter and lame metre; graced indeed since by the use of some famous modern poets, carried away by custom, but much to their own vexation, hindrance, and constraint to express many things otherwise, and for the most part worse, than else they would have expressed them."

The chief arguments against rime are those mentioned by Milton, its tendency to conceal "wretched matter and lame metre," and the necessity it often forces upon poets of either twisting unpleasantly what they have to say or of adding irrelevant matter. Besides these there is also what Cowper called "clock-work tintinnabulum" — mere empty jingle. But all the arguments are double-edged. For although many inferior poets have imposed for a while on readers and critics by the superficial melody of rime alone, "wretched matter and lame metre" were never long successfully concealed by it. And although, as Hobbes wrote, rime "forces a man sometimes for the stopping of a chink to say something he did never think," it is a fact nevertheless that the second thought, induced by rime-necessity, "the rack of truest wits," [1] is sometimes if not better than the first, at least a worthy and hand-some brother to it. Whether rime be a hindrance, vexation, and constraint to the poet depends almost wholly on his mastery of the technique of verse. It is not always easier to write in unrimed measures, for, as Milton proudly implied, good blank verse is the most difficult of all metres. And although the jingle of like sounds may become tedious and mechanical if un-skilfully handled — "to all judicious ears trivial and of no true musical delight," says Milton again — it has also proved a source of richness and beauty of sound; and it should never be forgotten that in the true æsthetic judgment of poetry sound plays a very important part. [2]

The satisfaction which the ear receives from rime at the end of a verse has been aptly compared to the pleasure we feel when a long arch of melody returns to the dominant and then the tonic. More elaborate is

---

[1] See the whole of Ben Jonson's Fit of Rhyme against Rhyme.

[2] Compare Flaubert's extreme statement: "that a beautiful verse with-out meaning is superior to one that has meaning but is less beautiful."

Oscar Wilde's praise of rime — "that exquisite echo which in the music's hollow hill creates and answers its own voice; rhyme, which in the hands of a real artist becomes not merely a material element of metrical beauty, but a spiritual element of thought and passion also, waking a new mood, it may be, or stirring a fresh train of ideas, or opening by mere sweetness and suggestion of sound some golden door at which the Imagination itself had knocked in vain; rhyme, which can turn man's utterance into the speech of the gods; rhyme, the one chord we have added to the Greek lyre."

The real problem in the arguments on rime is its fitness or unfitness in particular kinds of poetry. No rules or laws can be formulated; men have judged differently at different times; but it has been generally felt that shorter poems, inasmuch as they are in a way the concentrated essence of poetry, and must make their full impression almost instantaneously, require all the advantages of the poetic art. Tennyson's unrimed lyrics and Collins' Ode to Evening are unusual, though successful, experiments. For long poems, however, there is not this necessity of immediate effect. Here rime is sometimes a vexation, sometimes not. Justification lies in special circumstances. The classical French drama found it indispensable; English poetic drama gave it a trial in the seventeenth century and rejected it. Narrative poems which contain a large lyrical element, like the Faerie Queene and the Eve of St. Agnes, are, all agree, enhanced by the rime. But no one would now wish to have Paradise Lost in rimed verse, though it is clear from the publisher's note in 1668 that many readers at the time were 'stumbled' because it was not. On the other hand, we feel that Chapman's and Pope's Homer and Dryden's Virgil might have been better without rimes. Once more, it lies with the poet — and with the poem — to justify his use of rime or his refusal of it; if he is a good poet and his judgment is not warped by local or temporary conditions there will rarely be any doubt.

Rimes are called *masculine* when they consist of one syllable, as *cries: arise; feminine* when they consist of two or more syllables, as *heedless: needless, beautiful: dutiful*. When both vowel and following consonant agree the rime is called *perfect*, as *might: right, solemn: column*. When the preceding consonant as well as the vowel and following consonant agree the rime is called *identical* or *echo* rime, as *reed: read, perfection: infection, ours: hours*. When there is a difference either in the vowel sound or in the following consonantal sound, that is, when assonance or consonance is substituted for rime, the rime is usually said to be approximate or imperfect, as *worth: forth, was: pass, gusht: dust* (Coleridge). When the rime words look alike but are pronounced differently, they are called *eye rimes*, as *war: car, brow: glow*. Sometimes false rimes occur which have no similarity of sound or appearance, but are more or less sanctioned by earlier pronunciation or by custom, as *high: humanity*. Sometimes also unaccented syllables are rimed with accented syllables, as *burning: sing*.

Imperfect rimes of all sorts are used for various reasons. Compared with some languages, English is not very rich in rime words; and for many words which poets are prone to use, such as *love, God, heaven,* etc., few available rimes exist. When good rimes are few, older pronunciations are often resorted to, as the familiar *love: move, blood: stood, north: forth.* In reading the older poets we find many rimes which are now imperfect but were once entirely correct, as the eighteenth century *fault: thought, join: shine, tea: way.* On the other hand, the poet's carelessness or indifference is sometimes to blame for approximate rimes, as Gray's *beech: stretch* in the Elegy, and his *relies: requires,* Blake's *lamb: name* and *tomb: come,* Coleridge's *forced: burst,* Whittier's notorious *pen: been,* etc. But to dogmatize on a point like this is obviously very dangerous. Certain poets, especially among the moderns, may be said to choose imperfect rimes deliberately, both as a fresh means of securing variety and avoiding the monotony of hackneyed rimes, and also as a means of subtly suggesting the imperfection and futility of life. A few famous examples, defensible and indefensible, are: Wordsworth's *robin: sobbing, sullen: pulling;* Tennyson's *with her: together, valleys: lilies;* Keats's *youths: soothe, pulse: culls;* Swinburne's *lose him: bosom: blossom.* Keats and Rossetti are noted for their free use of approximate rimes. The humorous rimes of Byron and Browning, among others, are of course in a different category.

Feminine rimes have been frequently rejected as undignified. They are, said Coleridge, "a lower species of wit"; and he instanced, not very justly, the couplet of Smart:

Tell me, thou son of great Cadwallader!
Hast sent the hare? or hast thou swallowed her? [1]

But again the right justification is successful use, and no one will deny that Swinburne's double and triple rimes have greatly enriched his verse and revealed to others unused possibilities of metre. Such rimes as *grey leaf: bay-leaf* were practically a new thing in 1865.[2]

Too evasive for explanatory analysis, almost too delicate and impalpable even for descriptive comment, are many of the best musical effects of fine poetry. The poet's ear and his sixth prosodic sense enable him to make his verse a perfect vehicle of his meaning and emotion. He chooses an appropriate stanza for his poem, discovers an unguessed power in some common measure, makes the words hurry or deliberately holds them back, varying the tempo with the spirit of the words, gives the pattern an unusual twist when the idea is unusual, startles or soothes by the sound as well as by the intellectual content of his lines — and accomplishes all these metrical nuances, not with the whip-snapping of the ring-master, but with the consummate art that conceals art. When his prosodic effects are obvious they lose their power; we can see how the trick is done and we do not marvel. But when we feel vaguely the haunting quality of a melodious line or the perfect metrical rightness of a phrase without knowing *why* the melody haunts us or the phrase just fits, then we both marvel and applaud; then the poet's

[1] Triple rimes are naturally excellent for joco-serious purposes, like the celebrated *intellectual: henpecked you all, Timbuctoo: hymn book too, thin sand doubts: ins and outs*.   [2] Swinburne, Dedication, 1865.

gift, his divine authorization, is patent, and we recognize his superiority with awe.

Some of these effects have already been mentioned in the preceding paragraphs; but besides the 'tone-color' of assonance and consonance and rime proper there are also effects of pitch and of tempo and of repetition, and imitative effects, more or less concrete and explainable. It is true that many trained readers find subtleties of sound and suggestiveness where others find none, and also that many find rich beauties that the poet himself was not aware of and did not intend. This latter case may be accounted for in two ways: sometimes a reader is supersubtle and imagines embellishments that do not exist; and sometimes the poet builds better than he knows. His intuition, or inspiration, or whatever one chooses to call it, endows him with powers of whose complete functioning he is not at the time conscious. As readers must steer carefully between these two dangers, so also the poet has to avoid on the one hand repelling us by the appearance of a metrical device and on the other losing an effect which he intends but which may be too delicate to be seen or felt. No one probably ever missed the simple melody of Poe's

> The viol, the violet, and the vine;

or the imitative effectiveness of Swinburne's

> With lisp of leaves and ripple of rain;

and though these beauties are obvious they are for most tastes not too obtrusive. But Tennyson's

> Low on the sand and loud on the stone

is not so obvious, and there is danger of its escaping notice. One hears the line with increased pleasure after the imitation of sound is pointed out; but only the trained ear catches it at first.

This correspondence of sound and sense is called *onomatopoeia*. It may appear in a single word, as *buzz*, *whack*, *crackle*, *roar*, etc.; or a combination of imitative words, as Tennyson's

> The moan of doves in immemorial elms,
> And murmuring of innumerable bees;

or a suggestive echo rather than direct imitation, as Shelley's

> Makes faint with too much sweet these heavy-wingèd thieves;

or a suggestion of motion rather than of sound, as Milton's sea-fish

> huge of bulk,
> Wallowing unwieldy, enormous in their gait,

and the

> Leviathan, which God of all his works
> Created hugest that swim the ocean stream;

or an attempt to imitate the motion described, as Tennyson's picture of Excalibur when Sir Bedivere hurls it into the lake —

> The great brand
> Made lightnings in the splendour of the moon,
> And flashing round and round, whirled in an arch,
> Shot like a streamer of the northern morn;

and Swinburne's more simple

> As a lamp
> Burns and bends all its blowing flame one way;

or even the correspondence of a harsh line and a harsh thought, as Browning's famous

Irks care the crop-full bird, frets doubt the maw-crammed beast?[1]

Sometimes there is obtained an effect of altered tempo; of which the best illustration, though hackneyed, is still Pope's clever couplets in the Essay on Criticism —

> When Ajax strives some rock's vast weight to throw,
> The line too labours, and the words move slow:
> Not so, when swift Camilla scours the plain,
> Flies o'er th' unbending corn, and skims along the main.[2]

Examples of similar metrical skill may be found everywhere, especially among the more conscious literary artists, such as Shelley, Tennyson, Rossetti, Swinburne, and Browning, too. A few worth study follow:

> To-morrow and to-morrow and to-morrow
> Creeps in this petty pace from day to day.
> > SHAKESPEARE, Macbeth, V, v.

> To bellow through the vast and boundless deep.
> > MILTON, Paradise Lost, I, 177.

> — Mixt
> Confus'dly, and which thus must ever fight.
> > Ibid., II, 913 f.

---

[1] For an extreme example of mimicry, see Southey's Lodore.

[2] Lines 370 ff. Dr. Johnson's comment on this last line is curious: "The swiftness of Camilla is rather contrasted than exemplified. Why the verse should be lengthened to express speed, will not easily be discovered. In the dactyls, used for that purpose by the ancients, two short syllables were pronounced with such rapidity, as to be equal only to one long; they, therefore, naturally exhibit the act of passing through a long space in a short time. But the alexandrine, by its pause in the midst, is a tardy and stately measure; and the word ' unbending,' one of the most sluggish and slow which our language affords, cannot much accelerate its motion."

So he with difficulty and labour hard
Mov'd on, with difficulty and labour he.
                    Paradise Lost, II, 1021 f.

Yielded with coy submission, modest pride,
And sweet reluctant amorous delay.   Ibid., IV, 310 f.

See how he lies at random, carelessly diffused,
With languished head unpropt,
As one past hope, abandoned,
And by himself given over.
                    MILTON, Samson Agonistes, 118 ff.

With doubtful feet and wavering resolution.
                    Ibid., 732

Some rousing motions in me, which dispose
To something extraordinary my thoughts.   Ibid., 1382 f.

And ten low words oft creep in one dull line.
                    POPE, Essay on Criticism, 347.

The broad and burning moon lingeringly arose.
                    SHELLEY, The Sunset.

Rugged and dark, winding among the springs.
                    SHELLEY, Alastor, 88.

Here, where precipitate Spring, with one light bound.
                    LANDOR, Fiesolan Idyl.

Hammering and clinking, chattering stony names.
                    TENNYSON, The Princess, III, 361.

Myriads of rivulets, hurrying through the lawn.
                    Ibid., VII, 205.

The league-long roller thundering on the reef.
                    TENNYSON, Enoch Arden, 580.

Then Philip standing up said falteringly.
                    Ibid., 283.

A long street climbs to one tall-tower'd hill.
                    Ibid., 5.

Clang battle-axe and clash brand.
                    TENNYSON, The Coming of Arthur, 492.

The blind wave feeling round his long sea-hall
In silence.   TENNYSON, Merlin and Vivien, 230 f.

Immingled with heaven's azure waveringly.
                                        TENNYSON, Gareth, 914.

The hoof of his horse slipt in the stream, the stream . . .
                                        Ibid., 1020.

The brooks of Eden mazily murmuring.
                                        TENNYSON, Milton.

And in the throbbing engine room
Leap the long rods of polished steel.
                                        OSCAR WILDE, La Mer.

Something has already been said above on the nature
and effects of pitch in spoken rhythm (pages 35 ff.). It
is a constant factor of language, but its usual function
is special emphasis or intensification. By itself it rarely
dominates or determines the rhythm. And since the
regular determinants of spoken rhythm are time and
stress, it follows of course that pitch serves usually to
reinforce these determinants.[1] But not always; for not
only does pitch sometimes clash with rhythmic stress,
but also it is sometimes a substitute for it. All three
of these functions — strengthening, opposing, and replacing stress — are operative in verse.
     In Shelley's line

          Laugh with an inextinguishable laughter,

a great deal of the effect is due to the combination of
word accent and emphatic pitch in the syllable -ting-,
so that not merely the one word but the one syllable
dominates the whole verse. In such frequent conflicts
of stress as "on the blue surface," where the prose

[1] It is not to be understood, however, that the higher the pitch the
greater the emphasis; for the contrary is often the case.

rhythm is ⏑⏑ ′ ′ ⏑ while the verse pattern has
⏑ ⏌ ⏑ ⏌ ⏑, the so-called hovering accent (as it is usually
described, with the theory that somehow the normal
quantity of stress is divided between *the* and *blue*) is
properly a circumflex accent, which in other words
means pitch. Similarly in "If I were a dead leaf," the
peculiar rhythm is to be explained as a balance of pitch
against stress. And in that metrically notorious line of
Tennyson's —

> Take your own time, Annie, take your own time.
> TENNYSON, Enoch Arden, 463.

the chief irregularity or dissonance is the clash of pitch
against stress in " own time." If the line read —

> So you're on time, Annie, so you're on time,

there would be an unusual arrangement of stresses and
unstressed syllables, a peculiar syncopation, but no
great difficulty.[1] Much simpler and clearer is the conflict of stress and pitch in such passages as

> Pansies, lilies, kingcups, daisies,
> Let *them* live upon *their* praises.
> WORDSWORTH, To the Small Celandine.[2]

---

[1] It is perhaps useless to debate about this line. Whether one divides
thus:

$$⏌ ⏑ \mid ⏑ ⏌ \mid ⏌ ⏑ \mid ⏌ ⏑ \mid ⏑ ⏌$$

and says there is an ' inversion ' in the first, third, and fourth feet, or
preferably thus:

$$\wedge ⏌ \mid ⏑ ⏑̆ ⏌ \mid \wedge ⏌ \mid ⏑ ⏌ \mid ⏑ ⏑̆ ⏌$$

the rhythm is extraordinary; and the added complexity of ' own ' puts it
entirely *hors concours*. Compare with it, however, Milton's

> Which but th' Omnipotent none could have foil'd.
> Paradise Lost, I, 273.
> Not merely titular, since by degree. Ibid., V, 774.

[2] The italics are not Wordsworth's.

> *I* only stirred in this black spot;
> *I* only lived — *I* only drew
> The accursèd breath of dungeon-dew.
>
> BYRON, Prisoner of Chillon.[1]

and Keats's

> Heard melodies are sweet, but those unheard.

and Marvel's

> Annihilating all that's made
> To a green thought in a green shade.

The most interesting, and the rarest, effect of pitch in verse is its use as a substitute for stress. In the much-discussed first line of Paradise Lost —

> Of man's first disobedience and the fruit,

there is a metrical stress on *dis-* of "disobedience." This is not so much, however, an intensification of an already existent secondary accent, as in, for example, Shelley's

> The eager hours and *un*reluctant years.
>
> Ode to Liberty, xi.

as the substitution of pitch for stress.[2] The adaptability of language to metre appears very clearly in such a line as Paradise Lost, III, 130 —

> Self-tempted, self-deprav'd: Man falls deceiv'd,

in which the first compound shows a conflict of pitch and stress (' self ' having a pitch-accent, but occurring in an unstressed part of the line), while the second shows pitch taking the place of stress. The whole line,

---

[1] Here the italics are the poet's.

[2] Some readers take the line thus:

◡ /̄ /̄ ◡ ◡ /̄ ◡ ◡̆ ◡ ◡ /̄

with emphasis or pitch-accent on ' first '; in which case the above explanation does not hold.

and indeed the whole passage, though not of high
poetic value, is an admirable illustration of the Miltonic freedom of substitution and syncopation —
pitch playing a very important rôle. One should read
the lines first as prose, with full emphasis on the expressive contrasts; then merely as verse, beating out the
metre regardless of the meaning; finally, with mutual
sacrifice and compromise between the two readings,
producing that exquisite adjustment which is the
characteristic of good verse. There is a similar example
of pitch and stress in the familiar

> What recks it them? what need they?   *They* are sped.

Repetition is a rhetorical not a metrical device,
though it is employed with great effectiveness in verse
as well as in prose:

> For Lycidas is dead, dead ere his prime,
> Young Lycidas . . .

> The leaves they were crispèd and sere —
> The leaves they were withering and sere.

But a frequent kind of repetition which is truly a
prosodic phenomenon and which, though primarily an
element of stanzaic form, has often an effect analogous
to those just described, is the refrain. This may vary
from the simple "My Mary" of Cowper's poem (see
page 103, above) to the elaboration of such a stanza as
Rossetti's Sister Helen:

> " Why did you melt your waxen man,
>   Sister Helen?
> To-day is the third since you began."
> " The time was long, yet the time ran,
>   Little brother."
>   (*O Mother, Mary Mother,*
> *Three days to-day, between Hell and Heaven!*)

in which the second, fifth, and sixth lines remain the same throughout the forty-two stanzas, and the second half of the last line as well.

Besides the prosodic variations and subtleties so far discussed, there are a great many peculiar rhythms, that is, unusual but harmonious changes from the set metrical pattern, modulations, adjustments and combinations of different melodies, which enormously enrich the verse of a poem. As in music the ear at length tires of the familiar harmonies too often repeated, so the precise regularity of the metrical pattern too closely followed becomes tedious and almost demands variety. To be sure, a certain amount of variety results of necessity from the continual adaptation of ordinary language to the requirements of verse; but many of the examples of early heroic couplets and early blank verse are enough to show that this natural variety is too slight to satisfy the ear. The poet must exert a perpetual vigilance to prevent monotony. But on the other hand, only the highly cultivated ear appreciates the very unusual subtleties of rhythm, and the poet must therefore, unless he is willing to deprive himself of ordinary human comprehension and write esoterically for the "fit audience though few" (in Milton's proud phrase), limit himself to reasonably intelligible modulations. "It is very easy to see," says Mr. Robert Bridges, "how the far-sought effects of the greatest master in any art may lie beyond the general taste. In rhythm this is specially the case; while almost everybody has a natural liking for the common fundamental rhythms, it is only after long familiarity

with them that the ear grows dissatisfied, and wishes
them to be broken; and there are very few persons indeed who take such a natural delight in rhythm for its
own sake that they can follow with pleasure a learned
rhythm which is very rich in variety, and the beauty of
which is its perpetual freedom to obey the sense and
diction." [1] Some examples of these finer rhythms, in
addition to the particular forms already given —
rhythms not altogether ' learned,' but occasionally far-
sought and peculiarly delicate — may be profitably
examined. One should keep the metrical pattern constantly in mind as a test or touchstone of the variations. To classify or arrange these illustrations in
special groups is difficult because so often the same line
exemplifies more than one sort of variation, but the
following more or less vague classes of modulation
(substitution and syncopation) may be differentiated,
and other peculiarities mentioned in passing.

The normal blank verse line calls for five stressed
syllables and five unstressed syllables; but when two
light syllables are naturally and easily uttered in the
time of one, trisyllabic feet occur, sometimes with and
sometimes without special effect —

> And pointed out those arduous paths they trod.
> > POPE, Essay on Criticism, I, 95.
> The cataracts blow their trumpets from the steep.
> > WORDSWORTH, Immortality Ode.
> Departed from thee; and thou resembl'st now.
> > MILTON, Paradise Lost, IV, 839.
> To quench the drouth of Phebus; which as they taste.
> > MILTON, Comus, 66.

[1] Milton's Prosody, p. 30 (ed.1901).

When this extra syllable comes at the end of the line it is more noticeable; for if it is a weak syllable, it tends to give the line a falling rhythm, and if it is a heavy syllable, it distinctly lengthens the line, with a semi-alexandrine effect —

> Of rebel angels, by whose aid aspiring.
> MILTON, Paradise Lost, I, 38.

> Remember who dies with thee, and despise death.
> FLETCHER, Valentinian, V, i.

Sometimes there are two consecutive lines having such hypermetrical syllables —

> Extolling patience as the truest fortitude;
> And to the bearing well of all calamities.
> MILTON, Samson Agonistes, 654 f.

Much more frequent, however, is the trisyllabic effect in which the number of syllables of a line remains constant, that is, in the heroic or 5-stress line does not exceed ten —

> Infinite wrath and infinite despair.
> MILTON, Paradise Lost, IV, 74.

> Suddenly flashed on her a wild desire.
> TENNYSON, Lancelot and Elaine, 355.

And the following line (Comus, 8) contains an extra syllable at the end, one in the middle, and also a trisyllabic effect at the beginning —

> Strive to keep up a frail and feverish being.

This last phenomenon, the trisyllabic (or dactylic, or anapestic) effect, is commonly described as an inversion — the ' rule ' being given that in certain parts of the line the iamb is *inverted* and becomes a trochee.

This explanation is convenient, but it is open to the objection of inaccuracy. It almost stands to reason that when a rising rhythm is established the sudden reversal of it would produce a harsh discordant effect, would practically destroy the rhythmic movement for the time being. So it is in music, at any rate,[1] whereas it is not so with these ' inverted feet ' of verse. Therefore it seems more reasonable to scan such a line as that of Tennyson thus:

> ∧ Sud | denly flashed | on her | a wild | desire,

and the substitution is simply that of a triple rising (anapestic) for a duple rising (iambic) rhythm in the same time. *Sud-* is a monosyllabic foot, and the preceding rest is easily accounted for by the pause at the end of the previous line. In fact, this phenomenon is nearly always in immediate proximity to a pause either at the beginning of a line or in the middle. Very common is the movement —

> Flashing thick flames, wheel within wheel withdrawn.
> > MILTON, Paradise Lost, VI, 751.

> Thou on whose stream, 'mid the steep sky's commotion.
> > SHELLEY, Ode to the West Wind.

> Or if they sing, 'tis with so dull a cheer
> That leaves look pale, dreading the Winter's near.
> > SHAKESPEARE, Sonnet 97.

Less simple are the following lines from Samson Agonistes —

> The mystery of God, given me under pledge.   378.
> With goodness principl'd not to reject.   760.
> The jealousy of love, powerful of sway.   791.
> To satisfy thy lust: love seeks to have love.   837.

---

[1] The pronounced syncopations of ragtime partially illustrate this.

Still more unusual are —

> Yet fell: remember and fear to transgress.
>> Paradise Lost, VI, 912.
> Of thrones and mighty seraphim prostrate.
>> Ibid., VI, 841.

But in the last example Milton's pronunciation would give the second syllable of ' prostrate ' a weak accent to support the metrical stress. That he was willing to take the extreme risk, however, and actually invert the rhythm of the last foot, appears from unequivocal instances in Paradise Lost:

> Which of us who beholds the bright surface. VI, 472.
> Beyond all past example and future. X, 840.

In a short poem such lines as these last would presumably be unthinkable; probably Milton counted on the length of Paradise Lost to fix the rhythm so securely in the reader's ear that even this bold departure from the normal would seem a welcome relief. But it is both notable and certain that in a lyric measure the very same inversion does not seem unpleasantly dissonant —

> I'm sittin' on the stile, Mary,
>> Where we sat side by side
> On a bright May mornin' long ago,
>> When first you were my bride.
> The corn was springin' fresh and green,
>> And the lark sang loud and high,
> And the red was on your lip, Mary,
>> And the love-light in your eye.
>> LADY DUFFERIN, Lament of the Irish Emigrant.

Allied to this practice of inversion, or apparent inversion, are two other phenomena: the deliberate violation of normal word-accent to fit the metrical stress,[1] and an analogous violation of phrasal stress. The former is not such an entirely arbitrary procedure as it might at first seem; for at one period in the history of the language the accent of many words (especially those of French origin) was uncertain. Chaucer could say, without forcing, either *náture* or *natúre*. The revival of English poetry in the sixteenth century owed a great deal to Chaucerian example, and thus a tradition of variable accent was accepted and became practically a convention, not limited to those words in which it had originally occurred. Parallels to Milton's "but extreme shift" (Comus, 273) are very frequent in Spenser and Shakespeare: the rhythm is not ∪ ⊥ ∪ ⊥ nor ∪ ∪ ⊥ ⊥ but a sort of compromise between the two. So in Shelley's To a Skylark —

> In *profuse* strains of unpremeditated art,

and in verse of all kinds.

The wrenching of accent for metrical purposes, moreover, is not confined to the dissyllabic words which show the simple recession of accent. Some poets, especially the moderns (among others, Rossetti and Swinburne) have deliberately forced the word accent to conform to the metrical pattern in a way that can scarcely be called adaptation or adjustment; that is to say, the irregularities cannot successfully be ' organized ' by syncopation and substitution so as to produce a true rhythmic movement. For example —

---

[1] In the specific cases mentioned below, this phenomenon is historically known as "recession of accent"; and it sometimes occurs in non-metrical contexts. It is also very similar to one of the aspects of pitch; see pages 181 f., above.

> But coloured leaves of latter rose-blossom,
> Stems of soft grass, some withered red and some
> Fair and fresh-blooded, and spoil splendider
> Of marigold and great spent sunflower.
>   SWINBURNE, The Two Dreams.

So Keats has —

> The enchantment that afterwards befell.

Those whose taste sanctions such *outré* effects probably find pleasure in the strangeness and daring of the
rhythm.

An analogous case to this distributed stress but with
monosyllables instead of polysyllabic words is the
familiar line in Lycidas —

> The hungry sheep look up and are not fed.

One does not read: "but *are* not *fed*," nor "but are *not
fed*," but rather something midway between. This variation, common with all poets, was a special favorite of
Shelley's —

> To deck with their bright hues his withered hair.
>   . . . His eyes beheld
> Their own wan light through the reflected lines
> Of his thin hair, distinct in the dark depth
> Of that still fountain. . . .
> Mingling its solemn song, whilst the broad river.
>   Alastor.

The monosyllabic foot in which the unstressed element is missing offers no difficulty. The familiar example of

> Break, break, break,

has been discussed above (pages 63 f.). Compare also
Tennyson's Sweet and Low; Fletcher's song —

> Lay a garland on my hearse
>   Of the dismal yew;
> Maidens, willow branches bear;
>   Say, I died true;

and Yeats's —

> We sat grown quiet at the name of love;
> We saw the last embers of daylight die.
>
> Adam's Curse.

Shelley has —

> And wild roses and ivy serpentine.
>
> The Question.

and Swinburne —

> Fragrance of pine-leaves and odorous breath.
>   Song for the Centenary of Walter Savage Landor.

(where it would be absurd to make two syllables of "pine"), and a debated but perfectly intelligible hexameter —

> Full-sailed, wide-winged, poised softly forever asway.

where the whole music of the line depends upon giving due time-emphasis to "poised." There is one odd case, not to be made too much of because one cannot be entirely sure of the text, in Shakespeare's Measure for Measure, II, ii, of the omission of the stressed element of a foot —

> Than the soft myrtle; ∧ but man, proud man.

The versification of the whole play, however, is peculiar, and this metrical anomaly may have been deliberate.

The older writers on versification, leaning heavily on the traditional prosody of Greek and Latin, made much of the cæsura or pause, especially in blank verse.

As has already been frequently suggested, the varied placing of the pause is one of the commonest means of avoiding monotony and giving freedom and fluency to the verse, but it is often also a means of fitting the verse to the meaning. Since the pause comes most frequently near the middle of the line, when it occurs within the first or the last foot there is some special emphasis intended, as in Milton's —

> Before him, such as in their souls infix'd
> Plagues.   Paradise Lost, VI, 837 f.
>
>   Last
> Rose as in dance the stately trees, and spread.
>   Ibid., VII, 323 f.

For Milton these were rather bold and unusual. Later poets have made them familiar, but no less effective. Note Swinburne's repeated use in Atalanta in Calydon —

> His helmet as a windy and withering moon
> Seen through blown cloud and plume-like drift, when ships
> Drive, and men strive with all the sea, and oars
> Break, and the beaks dip under, drinking death.[1]

Except in these two places, however, there is seldom a very particular effect sought. That there can be even a good deal of regularity without stiffness or monotony is plain from a passage like Paradise Lost, II, 344 ff.[2] The presence of several pauses in a line produces a broken, halting, retarded effect, as —

---

[1] Note also the spondaic effect in the second line, the rime in the third, and the imitative movement in the fourth.

[2] Here, dividing the lines into parts measured by the number of syllables, the series is: 6+4, 6+4, —, 2+4+4, 6+4, 8+2, 6+4, 6+4, 6+4, 8+2, 8+2, etc.

> Through wood, through waste, o'er hill, o'er dale, his roam.
>
> Paradise Lost, IV, 538.

and is admirably used by Milton in describing Satan's arduous flight through Chaos —

> O'er bog or steep, through strait, rough, dense, or rare,
> With head, hands, wings, or feet, pursues his way,
> And swims, or sinks, or wades, or creeps, or flies.
>
> Paradise Lost, II, 948 ff.

Theoretically each rhythmic stress is of equal force or strength, but in verse there is the greatest variety, some stresses being so strong as to dominate a whole line, others so light as hardly to be felt. Thus it happens sometimes that in a 5-stress line there are actually only four or three stresses: the rhythmic result being a syncopation of four or three against five. Sometimes the word which contains the weak stress receives unusual emphasis, as —

> Which if not victory is yet revenge.
>
> Paradise Lost, II, 105.

> Fall'n cherub, to be weak is miserable.
>
> Ibid., I, 157.

> Me miserable! which way shall I fly.
>
> Ibid., IV, 73.

> Low-seated she leans forward massively.
>
> THOMSON, City of Dreadful Night.

> Like earth's own voice lifted unconquerable.
>
> SHELLEY, Revolt of Islam, IX, 3.

Sometimes the emphasis seems distributed, as —

> As he our darkness, cannot we his light.
>
> Paradise Lost, II, 269.

> Passion and apathy and glory and shame.
>
> Ibid., II, 567.

Eyeless in Gaza at the mill with slaves.

> Samson Agonistes, 41.

Envy and calumny and hate and pain.

> Shelley, Adonais, xl.

And sometimes no special emphasis is apparent, as —

Servile to all the skyey influences.

> Shakespeare, Measure for Measure, III, i.

Like a sad votarist in palmer's weed.

> Milton, Comus, 189.

Gorgons and hydras and chimæras dire.

> Paradise Lost, II, 628.

But fooled by hope, men favor the deceit.

> Dryden.

The friar hooded and the monarch crowned.

By strangers honour'd and by strangers mourn'd.

> Pope.

With forest branches and the trodden weed.

> Keats.

The rhythm of the last four examples is very common in all English verse. Occasionally the metre becomes almost ambiguous — according to its metrical context the line may be either 4-stress or 5-stress, as —

To the garden of bliss, thy seat prepar'd.

> Paradise Lost, VIII, 299.

By the waters of life, where'er they sat.

> Ibid., IX, 79.

In the visions of God. It was a hill.

> Ibid., XI, 377.

Three-stress lines in blank verse are less frequent, but the more striking when they do occur. There is Shakespeare's famous —

To-morrow and to-morrow and to-morrow.

Milton's

                        Omnipotent,
        Immutable, immortal, infinite,
        Eternal King.   Paradise Lost, III, 372 ff.

(where the heaping up of the polysyllabic epithets adds
greatly to the effect); and

            Of difficulty or danger could deter.
                                  Paradise Lost, II, 499.

            Of happiness and final misery.   Ibid., II, 563.

            Abominable, inutterable, and worse.
                                        Ibid., II, 626.

            His ministers of vengeance and pursuit.
                                          Ibid., I, 170.

and Meredith's

            The army of unalterable law.
                                    Lucifer in Starlight.

and such lines as —

            Unrespited, unpitied, unreprieved.
                                  Paradise Lost, II, 185.

for which parallels may be found in several other poets
before and after Milton.

There is no reason why a metrically 5-stress line
should not contain only two prose stresses, but examples are of course rare. Such an unusual rhythm
would be seldom demanded. The phrase "acidulation
of perversity" might do, for it is easily modulated to
the metrical form. Occasionally, as in the last line of
Christina Rossetti's sonnet quoted on pages 120 f., a
series of monosyllables with almost level inflection will
reduce the prose emphasis of a line and force attention
on the important words —

        Than that you should *remember* and be *sad*.

A better example is Shelley's

> A sepulchre for its eternity.   Epipsychidion, 173.

In direct contrast to these lines whose effectiveness springs from a lack of the normal quantity of stress are those which are metrically overweighted. A single stressed monosyllable, supported or unsupported by a pause, may occupy the place of a whole rhythmic beat, or it may be compressed to the value of a theoretically unstressed element. Thus Milton's well-known line —

> Rocks, caves, lakes, fens, bogs, dens, and shades of death.
> Paradise Lost, II, 621.

might if it stood by itself equally well be taken as an 8-stress or as a 5-stress line; and obviously in a blank verse context it produces a very marked retardation of the tempo. No one would dream of reading it in the same space of time as the rapid line which just precedes it and to which it stands in such striking contrast —

> O'er many a frozen, many a fiery Alp.

Similar are —

> Light-armed, or heavy, sharp, smooth, swift or slow.
> Paradise Lost, II, 902.

> Stains the dead, blank, cold air with a warm shade.
> SHELLEY, Epipsychidion, 92.

> Of waves, flowers, clouds, woods, rocks, and all that we
> Read in their smiles, and call reality.   Ibid., 511 f.

> We have lov'd, prais'd, pitied, crown'd, and done thee wrong.
> SWINBURNE, On the Cliffs.

For extreme examples of the accelerandos and ritenutos which our metrical ear seems willing to accept easily,

one might compare two 4-stress lines by contemporary
poets —

> In the mystery of life.   ROBERT BRIDGES.

> On the highest peak of the tired gray world.
>   SARA TEASDALE.

or Swinburne's —

> The four boards of the coffin lid
> Heard all the dead man did. . . .

> The dead man asked of them:
> "Is the green land stained brown with flame?"
>   After Death.

These few general classifications by no means ex-
haust the possibilities of metrical variations and adjustments. In a real sense, every line is rhythmically
different from every other line; but many of these differences are subjective, that is, they are determined by
the individual training, tastes, habits, of each reader,
his familiarity with few or many poets, the physical
constitution of his organs of hearing, even the temporary mood in which he reads. The actual, objective
peculiarities of a line are always significant, if the poet
is a true master, but such is the variableness of experience and of life itself that unless we possess the
poet's understanding and his sensitiveness — or can
cultivate them — we lose a certain part of the significance. For one person, therefore, to dogmatize is
both impertinent and misleading: the following specimens of peculiar rhythm are accordingly left without
special comment. Some of them have long been bones
of contention among prosodists; some of them are almost self-explanatory, others are subtle and difficult

(and must be felt rather than explained), others have perhaps only their unusualness to recommend them to one's attention. In every case, however, they should be studied both in their metrical context and by themselves. They should be approached not only as technical problems in the accommodation of natural speech emphasis to the formal patterns of verse, but also — and this is the more important point of view — as adjustments in the second degree, adjustments of the prose-and-verse harmonies to the fullest expressiveness of which language is capable. It is a common observation that emotional language tends of itself to become rhythmical; the emotional and highly wrought language of poetry requires the restraint of verse as a standard by which its rhythms may be more powerfully realized and its significant deviations therefrom measured. And it is almost a constant ' law ' that the more acute or profound the emotion, the more complex is the rhythm which gives it fit and adequate expression in words. ' Complex ' does not necessarily mean arcane or supersubtle or *recherché*. On the contrary, simplification (though not simplicity) is one of the characteristics of the best and greatest art. But to simplify beyond a certain point the various entangled implications of a poignant emotion is merely to rob it of some of its fundamental qualities. Nor is it childish to reason that a peculiar or extraordinary idea is most naturally expressed by a peculiar or extraordinary rhythm. Argument aside, it is an observable and verifiable fact.

That we may so suffice his vengeful ire.
> MILTON, Paradise Lost, I, 148.

A mind not to be changed by time or place.
> Ibid., I, 253.

Behold me then, me for him, life for life.
> Ibid., III, 236.

Both God and Man, Son both of God and Man.
> Ibid., III, 316.

As from blest voices, uttering joy, Heav'n rung.
> Ibid., III, 347.

Infinite wrath and infinite despair.   Ibid., IV, 74.

Raphael, the sociable spirit, that deign'd.
> Ibid., V, 221.

Of truth, in word mightier than they in arms.
> Ibid., VI, 32.

Before thy fellows, ambitious to win.
> Ibid., VI, 160.

On me already lost, me than thyself
More miserable.   Both have sinned; but thou
Against God only; I against God and thee.
> Ibid., X, 929 ff.

O miserable mankind, to what fall.
> Ibid., XI, 500.

And made him bow to the gods of his wives.
> Paradise Regained, II, 171.

Hail, Son of the Most High, heir of both worlds.
> Ibid., IV, 633.

Wilt thou then serve the Philistines with that gift?
> Samson Agonistes, 576.

Thea! Thea! Thea! where is Saturn?
> KEATS, Hyperion, I, 134.

When night makes a weird sound of its own stillness.
> SHELLEY, Alastor, 30.

Yielding one only response, at each pause.
> SHELLEY, Alastor, 564.

Touch, mingle, are transfigured; ever still
Burning, yet ever inconsumable.
> SHELLEY, Epipsychidion, 578 f.

Lies to God, lies to man, every way lies.
> BROWNING, The Ring and the Book, IV, 216.

'Do I live, am I dead?' Peace, peace seems all.
> BROWNING, The Bishop Orders his Tomb.

Good strong thick stupefying incense-smoke.
> Ibid.

I cry 'Life!' 'Death,' he groans, 'our better life!'
> BROWNING, Aristophanes' Apology, 1953.

Setebos, Setebos, and Setebos.
> BROWNING, Caliban upon Setebos.

Even to the last dip of the vanishing sail.
> TENNYSON, Enoch Arden, 244.

Saying gently, Annie, when I spoke to you.
> Ibid., 445.

Palpitated, her hand shook, and we heard.
> TENNYSON, The Princess, IV, 389.

Bearing all down, in thy precipitancy.
> TENNYSON, Gareth, 8.

First as in fear, step after step, she stole
Down the long tower stairs, hesitating.
> TENNYSON, Lancelot and Elaine, 342 f.

This from Surrey's Æneid, because of its early date:

He with his hands strave to unloose the knots.

These two from Elizabethan drama — hundreds of interesting lines may be culled from this source, but the field is to be trodden with caution because of the uncertainties of the texts; though we quote 'Hamlet' we

cannot be sure we are quoting Shakespeare, and in
such a matter as this *certainty* is indispensable —

> Do more than this in sport. — Father, father.
>> King Lear, II, i.

> Cover her face; mine eyes dazzle; she died young.
>> Webster, Duchess of Malfi, IV, ii.

And finally, three examples from Samson Agonistes
of interwoven tunes, a sort of counterpoint of two
melodies sounding simultaneously —

> My griefs not only pain me
> As a lingering disease,
> But, finding no redress, ferment and rage.   617 ff.

>> To boast
> Again in safety what thou would'st have done
> To Samson, but shalt never see Gath more.   1127 ff.

>> Force with force
> Is well ejected when the conqueror can.   1206 f.

> He all their ammunition
> And feats of war defeats,
> With plain heroic magnitude of mind.   1277 ff.

Stevenson compared the writer of verse with a juggler who cleverly keeps several balls in the air at one
time. The comparison is suggestive, but is true only
so far as it indicates the difficulty of the operation for
those who are not jugglers. The juggler does not devote conscious attention to each individual ball. He
has learned to keep them all moving at once, and when
he starts them they go *of their own accord*. Now and
then, by conscious effort, he shoots one higher than the
others — but there is no need to labor the illustration.
The technique of versification is a mechanical thing to

be learned like any mechanical thing. The poet learns it — in sundry different ways, to be sure — and when he has mastered it he is no more conscious of its complex details while he is composing than the pianist is conscious of his ten fingers while he is interpreting a Chopin concerto. There is a feeling, an idea, a poetic conception, which demands expression in words. The compound of direct intellectual activity and of automatic responses from a reservoir of intuitions long since filled by practice and experience no poet has ever been able to analyze — much less a psychologist who is not a poet. Often the best ideas, the best phrases, the perfect harmony of thought and expression *emerge* spontaneously; sometimes they have to be sought, diligently and laboriously sought.

"When one studies a prosody or a metrical form," says M. Verrier, "one may well ask if these alliterations, these assonances, these consonances, these rimes, these rhythmic movements, these metres, which one coldly describes in technical terms — if they actually produce the designated effects and especially if the poet ' thought of all that.' So it is when an amateur opens a scientific treatise on music and learns by what series of chords one modulates from one key to another, or even how the chord of the dominant seventh is resolved to the tonic in its fundamental form. . . . That the poet has not ' thought of all that ' is evident, but not in the ordinary sense. When the illiterate countryman makes use of the subjunctive, he is not aware that a subjunctive exists, still less that one uses it for historical and logical and also perhaps for emotional reasons. But the subjunctive exists nevertheless, and the reasons too." [1]

The analogy is helpful, though not altogether persuasive. There is the familiar story of Browning's reply to the puzzled admirer: "Madam, I have no idea what I meant when I wrote those lines." So much for warning to the oversedulous. But if I honestly find and feel a marvelous rhythmic effect where Robert Browning did not plan one, then such effect certainly exists — for me, at least, and for all whom I can persuade of its presence. On the other hand, there is a potent warning in the following exuberance:

But the thought of the king and his villainies stings him into rage again, and the rhythm slowly rises on three secondary stresses —

> or ere this
> I should have fatted all the region kites
> With this slave's offal.

The last phrase twists and writhes through a series of secondary stresses with an intensity of hatred and bitterness that takes shape in a following series of peculiar falling rhythm waves, each one of which has a foam-covered crest ' white as the bitten lip of hate.' This rhythm, curling, hissing, tense, topful of venom, Alecto's serpents coiling and twisting through it, makes one of the most awful passages in all English poetry —

> Bloody, bawdy villain!
> Remorseless, treacherous, lecherous, kindless villain!

and culminates in Hamlet's cry

> O vengeance!

which, with its peculiar sustained falling close, vibrates through the rest of the verse.[2]

---

[1] Verrier, vol. i, p. 134.
[2] Mark H. Liddell, An Introduction to the Scientific Study of English Poetry, New York, 1902, pp. 291 f.

Professional prosodists doubt and dispute one another with the zeal and confidence of metaphysicians
and editors of classical texts. They are all blind guides
— perhaps even the present one! — if followed slav-
ishly. There is only one means (a threefold unity) to
the right understanding of the metrical element in
poetry: a knowledge of the simple facts of metrical
form, a careful scrutiny of the existent phenomena of
ordinary language rhythms, and a study of the ways in
which the best poets have fitted the one to the other
with the most satisfying and most moving results.

GLOSSARIAL INDEX

GLOSSARIAL INDEX

A few terms not mentioned in the text are included here for the sake
of completeness.

ACCENT, the greater emphasis placed, in normal speech, on one syllable of a work as compared with the other syllables, 6, 34 f., 37 f. *See also* STRESS; it is convenient to distinguish the two terms, but they are sometimes used interchangeably.

ACEPHALOUS, headless; used to describe a line which lacks the unstressed element of the first foot. *See* TRUNCATION.

ALEXANDRINE, a 6-stress iambic line, 85 ff. 88.

ALLITERATION, repetition of the same or closely similar sounds at the beginning of neighboring words or accented syllables (occasionally also unaccented syllables); sometimes called *Initial Rime*, 166.

AMPHIBRACH, a classical foot, $\cup - \cup$, 51.

ANACRUSIS, one or more extra syllables at the beginning of a line, 71.

ANAPEST, a foot consisting of two unstresses and a stress, $\cup \cup \underline{}$, 38, 51, 70, 80 ff.

ANTISTROPHE, the counter-turn, or stanza answering to the first, of a Pindaric Ode, 131.

ARSIS, a confusing term sometimes borrowed from classical prosody for the stressed element of a foot; the unstressed element is called *Thesis*.

ASSONANCE, the repetition, in final syllables, of the same vowel sound followed by a different consonantal sound, 166 f. *See* RIME.

BALLAD METRE (Common Measure, C. M. of the Hymnals), the stanza $a^4b^3a^4b^3$, but admitting certain variations, 87, 103.

BALLADE, a formal metrical scheme of three stanzas riming *ababbcbC* with an Envoi *bcbC*, keeping the same rimes throughout, and the last line of each stanza (*C*) being the same. The lines are usually 5-stress, 163.

BLANK VERSE, unrimed 5-stress lines used continuously, 94, 133 ff., ch. V passim; the the 'single-moulded' line, 135 f.; Marlow's, 137 f.; Shakespeare's, 138 ff., later dramatic, 140 f.; Milton's, 142 ff.; conversational, 147 ff.

CAESURA, the classical term for a pause, usually grammatical and extra-metrical (i.e. not reckoned in the time scheme). When it follows an accented syllable it is called *masculine*; when it follows an unaccented syllable it is *feminine*; when it occurs within a line it is called *medial*; when it occurs after an 'extra' unstressed syllable it is called *epic* (though as frequent in drama as in epic), as —

> And earth's base built on stubble. | But come, let's on.
> MILTON, Comus, l. 599.

CATALEXIS; *see* TRUNCATION.

CHORIAMB, a classical foot, $-\cup\cup-$, 51.

COMMON MEASURE (C. M.), the regular *Ballad Metre*, 103 f.

CONSONANCE, specifically, in metrics, a form of incomplete rime in which the consonantal sounds agree but the vowel sounds differ, 166 f. *See* RIME.

COÖRDINATION, the agreement or coincidence of the natural prose rhythm with the metrical (rhythmical) pattern; the process of making them agree, 17 f.

COUPLET, a group of two lines riming *aa*, 88; *closed* couplet, one which contains an independent clause or sentence and does not run on into the next of the series, 91 f.; *heroic* couplet, one of 5-stress lines, usually iambic (called also *pentameter* couplet), 89, 93 ff.; *short* couplet, one of 4-stress iambic or trochaic lines (also called *octosyllabic* couplet), 89 ff.

DACTYL, a foot consisting of a stress followed by two unstresses, $-\cup\cup$, 38, 51, 70, 84.

DECASYLLABLE, a 5-stress (pentameter) line; a term used properly only of syllable-counting metres such as the French.

DISTICH, couplet; usually in classical prosody the elegiac couplet of a hexameter and a pentameter, 162.

DOGGEREL, any rough irregular metre.

DUPLE RHYTHM, a rhythm of two beats (though corresponding generally to $\frac{3}{4}$ time in music), one stress and one unstress, $-\cup$ or $\cup-$.

DURATION, the length of time occupied by the enunciation of speech-sounds, and therefore an element in all language rhythm, 5. *See also* TIME.

ELEGIAC STANZA, the quatrain *abab*[5], 103, 107 f.

ELISION, the omission or crowding out of unstressed words or unaccented syllables to make the metre smoother; a term belonging to classical prosody and inappropriate in English prosody except where syllable-counting verse is concerned. Various forms of Elision are called Syncope, Synizesis, and Synalœpha.

END-STOPPED LINE, one with a full or strong grammatical pause at the end.

ENJAMBEMENT, a French term ('long stride') for the continuation of the sense from one line (or couplet) to the next without a grammatical pause, 62, 92; opposite of End-stopping. *See* OVERFLOW; RUN-ON LINE.

EPODE, the third (sixth, ninth) stanza of a Pindaric ode, 131.

FEMININE ENDING, an extra unstressed syllable at the end of an iambic or anapestic line, 71.

FOOT, the smallest metrical unit of rhythm, composed of a stressed element and one or more unstressed elements (or a pause), 49 ff.

FREE-VERSE, irregular rhythms, not conforming to a fixed metrical pattern, 150 ff.

HEADLESS LINE, acephalous; and *see* TRUNCATION.

HENDECASYLLABLE, a 5-stress line with feminine ending, thus making ordinarily eleven syllables; usually referring to a special metre used by Catullus and others (as in Tennyson's imitation, 'O you chorus of indolent reviewers'), 162.

HEROIC LINE, a 5-stress iambic line.

HEXAMETER, *classical* or *dactylic*, the standard line of Greek and Latin poetry, composed of six feet, the fifth of which is nearly always a dactyl, the sixth a spondee or trochee, the rest either dactyls or spondees; imitated in English with more or less success by substituting stress for quantity, 159 ff.

HIATUS, unexpected absence of elision.

HOLD, pause on a word or syllable, 62 f.

HOVERING ACCENT, a term sometimes used for the coördination of the metrical rhythm $\cup\,\underline{}\,\cup\,\underline{}$ with the prose rhythm $\cup\,\cup\,\underline{}\,\underline{}$ as in "and serene air" (Comus, l. 4); the accent is thought of as 'hovering' over the first syllable of *serene*, 182.

HYPERMETRIC, used of a syllable which is not reckoned or expected in the regular metrical pattern.

IAMB, *Iambus*, a foot consisting of an unstress and a stress, $\cup\,\underline{}$, 38, 51, 69, 84 ff.

IN MEMORIAM STANZA, a quatrain riming *abba*⁴, 103, 105 ff.

INVERSION, the substitution of a trochee for an iamb or of a dactyl for an anapest (or vice versa), 51, 187 ff.; a misleading term; see SUBSTITUTION.

LENGTH, the comparative duration of the enunciation of syllables, 33 f. In classical prosody syllables were regarded by convention as either 'long' or 'short' (a 'long' being theoretically equal to two 'shorts'), and this usage has been sometimes (not successfully, and yet not entirely without reason) superimposed upon English verse.

LINE, a metrical division composed of one or more feet and either used continuously or combined in stanzas, 52 f., 69 ff. *See* VERSE (1).

LOUDNESS, the comparative strength or volume of a sound, 6.

LONG MEASURE (L. M. of the Hymnals) the quatrain riming *abab*⁴ or *abcb*⁴, 103.

METRE, a regular, artificial, rhythmic pattern, the formal basis of versification.

OCTOSYLLABLE, an 8-syllable or 4-stress line. *See* DECASYLLABLE.

OCTAVE, a stanza of eight lines; especially the two quatrains of an Italian sonnet, 120.

ODE, a kind of exalted lyric poem, not strictly a metrical term but often used as such to describe the simple stanzaic structure of the 'Horatian' ode or the complex system of strophe, antistrophe and epode of the 'Pindaric' ode, 131 ff.

ONOMATOPOEIA, primarily a rhetorical figure but of much wider application, covering all cases from single words to phrases and lines of verse in which there is agreement, by echo or suggestions, between the sound of the words and their meaning; as a metrical term, the agreement of the verse rhythm with the idea expressed, 177 ff.

OTTAVA RIMA, the stanza (of Italian origin) riming $ababab cc^5$, 111 f.

OVERFLOW, the running over of the parts of a sentence from one line to the next without a pause at the end of the line, 62. *See* ENJAMBEMENT, RUN-ON.

PAEON, a classical foot, $-\cup\cup\cup$, 51, 76 ff.

PAUSE, (1) *logical* or *grammatical*, that which separates the formal parts of a sentence, 61, 63; (2) *rhythmical*, that which separates the breath-groups of spoken sentences, 61 ff.; (3) *metrical*, (*a*) that which separates the parts of a metrical pattern, as at the end of a line, 62, and also (*b*) that which takes the place of an unstressed element of a foot, being equivalent to the rest in music (indicated by the sign $\wedge$), 62 ff.

PENTAMETER, a 5-stress line, 52. (This term is well established, but open to objection.)

PHRASE, a group of words held together either by their meaning (or content) or by their sound, 32 f., 37 ff.

PINDARIC, *see* ODE.

PITCH, the characteristic of a sound dependent upon its number of vibrations per second; (usually indicated by its place in the musical scale; high or 'acute,' low or 'grave'); 5 f., 35 ff.; sometimes functions in verse for emphasis or for stress, 8, 35 ff., 181 ff.

POULTER'S MEASURE, an old-fashioned couplet, composed of an alexandrine and a septenary, a^6a^7, 88 f.

PROSE, *Characteristic*, prose with natural and varied rhythms, 23 ff.; *Cadenced*, prose with carefully sought rhythmic movements, 27 ff.; *Metrical*, a hybrid of prose and verse, 29 ff.

PYRRHIC, a classical foot, $\cup\cup$, 51.

QUANTITY, the length of a syllable; established by convention in classical prosody; in English prosody very uncertain but always present. *See* LENGTH.

QUATRAIN, a stanza of four lines, 103 ff.

REFRAIN, a line or part of a line repeated according to the metrical pattern, 184 f.; the term *repetend* is occasionally used.

REST, *see* PAUSE (3, *b*).

RHYTHM, regular arrangement or repetition of varied parts, *see* ch. I, ch. II, and passim; *objective*, having external concrete existence, 3 ff.; *subjective*, felt by the individual, 3, 12 ff.;

spatial, in which the units are spaces, 4; *temporal*, in which the units are periods of time, 4 ff.; *rising*, beginning with the stressed element, 38; *falling*, beginning with the unstressed element, 38; *duple*, having a stress and one unstressed element (syllable), 38; *triple*, having a stress and two unstressed elements (syllables), 38.

RIME, repetition of the same sound (or sounds) usually at the end of the line, 165 ff.; *Masculine*, when the repeated sound consists of one stressed syllable; *Feminine*, when a stressed + one or more unstressed syllables; *Triple*, when a stressed + two unstressed syllables; *Echo* or *Identical*, when the preceding consonantal sound also agrees; *Eye-rime*, when the words agree in spelling but not in pronunciation, 174. As distinct from endrime, there is *Internal* or *Leonine* rime, which occurs within the line (sometimes merely a matter of printing). *See also* ASSONANCE, CONSONANCE.

RIME COUÉE, *see* TAIL-RIME STANZA.

RIME-ROYAL, a stanza borrowed by Chaucer from the French, *ababbcc*⁵; also called *Troilus stanza*, *Chaucer stanza*, 109 f.

RONDEAU, RONDEL, French metrical forms characterized by the repetition of the first phrase or lines twice as a refrain, e. g. *aabba aabR aabbaR* (R being the first phrase of the first line), or *ABba abAB abbaAB* (the capitals indicating the whole lines repeated), 163.

RUN-ON LINE, one in which the sense runs over into the following line without a grammatical pause, 62, 92. *See* ENJAMBEMENT; OVERFLOW.

SAPPHIC, a 4-line stanza used by Sappho (and Catullus and Horace) and often imitated in English; the pattern is $- \cup \,|$ $- \bar\cup\,|-\cup\cup\,|-\cup\,|-\cup$ thrice repeated, then $- \cup\cup\,|$ $- \cup$, 161 f.

SEPTENARY, SEPTENARIUS (fourteener), the old 14-syllable or 7-stress iambic line, later split up into the Ballad metre, 87; and used also with the alexandrine in the Poulter's Measure.

SESTET, a group of six lines, especially the last six of an Italian sonnet, 120.

SESTINA, an elaborate metrical form consisting of six 6-line stanzas and a 3-line stanza with repetition of the same end-words in different order instead of rime, 164.

SHORT MEASURE (S. M. of the Hymnals), the Poulter's Measure broken into a quatrain: $ab^3a^4b^3$, $ab^3c^4b^3$, 89.

SONNET, 118 ff., (1) *Italian*, a 14-line stanza composed of two quatrains riming *abba* and two tercets riming *cde cde* (*cde dce*, etc.), 120 ff.; (2) *English*, 14-line stanza of three quatrains riming *abab cdcd efef*, and a closing couplet *gg*, 127 ff. There are also mixed forms and many variations.

SPENSERIAN STANZA, a 9-line stanza riming *ababbcbc*⁵*c*⁶; the final alexandrine is the characteristic feature, 85 f., 112 ff. Several variations were used in the seventeenth century consisting of shorter lines with a closing alexandrine, 117.

SPONDEE, a classical prosody a foot of two long syllables; in English prosody a foot of two 'long' or accented or stressed words or syllables, 51.

STANZA, a group of lines arranged according to a special pattern, usually marked by rimes, 53, 88 ff.; *see also* VERSE (3).

STRESS, the comparative emphasis which distinguishes a sound from others not so strongly or plainly emphasized, 34 f., 37 f., 56 f., 65 f. Then by UNSTRESS or no stress is meant absence or comparative weakness of emphasis. *Stress* is used in this book for rhythmic and metrical emphasis; *see* ACCENT.

STROPHE, same as Stanza, 53; in the Pindaric ode, the first (fourth, etc.) stanza, 131.

SUBSTITUTION (1) replacing one rhythmic unit by its temporal equivalent, as an iamb by an anapest or by a trochee, etc., 20; called also *Inversion* (*q. v.*) of the foot; (2) the use of pitch or duration (pause) for a stress or unstress, 20, 181 ff.

SYLLABLE, the smallest and simplest unit of speech-sound, 32 f.; sometimes used as a metrical unit, 49.

SYNCOPATION, the union, or perception of the union, of two or more rhythmic patterns, 18 ff.

TAIL-RIME STANZA, one usually of six lines riming $aa^4b^3cc^4b^3$, but with many variations (e. g. the Burns stanza, $aaa^4b^2a^4b^2$), the general type being a combination of long lines in groups with single short lines, 109.

TAILED SONNET, a sonnet with a tail (coda), or addition. About the only one in English is Milton's On the New Forcers of Conscience: the rimes are *abba abba cde dec⁵ c³ff⁵f³gg⁵*.

TERCET, a group of three lines, especially in the sestet of the Italian sonnet, 102, 120.

TERZA RIMA, an Italian rime scheme *aba bcb cdc . . . yzy zz*; rarely used in English, but triumphantly (in stanzas) in Shelley's Ode to the West Wind, 164.

TETRAMETER, a classical term (four 'measures' or eight feet) incorrectly used for the English 4-stress line, 52.

THESIS, *see* ARSIS.

TIME, an inevitable element in English verse (as well as prose), but not the sole basis, 56 ff.

TONE-COLOR, TONE QUALITY, 'timbre,' the characteristic of a sound determined by the number of partial tones (overtones), as richness, sweetness, thinness, stridency; hence sometimes applied to the musical quality of a verse or phrase, 6 and note, 177.

TRIBRACH, a classical foot, ∪∪∪, 51.

TRIMETER, a classical term (three 'measures' or six feet) incorrectly used for the English 3-stress line, 52.

TRIOLET, a French metrical form, mainly for light themes, riming

ABAAABAB (the capitals indicating repeated lines) and usually with short lines, 163.

TRIPLET, a group of three lines, especially when rimed *aaa*, 102 f. *See also* TERCET.

TROCHEE, a foot consisting of a stress and an unstress, $\angle\cup$, 38, 51, 70, 82 ff.

TRUNCATION, omission of the final unstressed element of a line, usually in the trochaic metres, 76; also called *Catalexis* (the opposite of which, the non-omission of this element, is *Acatalexis*). *Initial Truncation* is the omission of the first unstressed element of a line, usually in the iambic metres, thus making a *Headless* verse.

UNSTRESS, the element of a rhythmic unit which is without emphasis or has a relatively weak emphasis.

VERSE, (1) a metrical line, 52; (2) collectively, for metre, metrical form; (3) commonly in England, and in America in the churches, used for Stanza.

VILLANELLE, a French verse form of nineteen lines on three rimes, certain lines being repeated at fixed intervals, 163 f.